Praise for _The Tra_

"_The Transformative_ _i_   tten
meditation on the art of human interaction. Huff writes from the
heart, not just the head. The book is easy to read, with practical
advice and an engaging wide range of stories about how to come
to agreement."

> —**_Natalie Goldberg_**, _bestselling author of_ Writing Down
> the Bones, Wild Mind, and The True Secret of Writing

"The skills covered in this precise volume will "transform"
both negotiated outcomes and the participants themselves.
Accomplished negotiator and attorney Michèle Huff draws
from Buddhist concepts of mindfulness, her personal business
experiences, and examples ranging from Nelson Mandela, Henry
Kissinger, and the Dalai Lama to explain core techniques that
work as well as those that do not. Simple exercises throughout
illustrate key concepts readers can make their own. From
awareness of physical aspects such as posture and breathing,
to controlling anger, and the sophisticated practice of humility,
these techniques will prove invaluable any time negotiation
partners need to come to agreement and in everyday life."

> —**_Marie Longserre_**, _CEO Santa Fe Business Incubator,_
> _former Board Chair National Business Incubation Association_

"Huff layers MBA level negotiation theory, lifelong experience, cross-cultural negotiation and practice of deeper wisdom in a series of clearly explained and immensely pragmatic examples. *The Transformative Negotiator* stresses the brain/body connection, our interdependence as human beings, as well as meditation techniques that lead to successful outcomes. It is a book you want to have handy in the midst of any negotiation from teenage kids to members of the board."

—*Miko Matsumura*, *Speaker, Silicon Valley Startup Advisor, Technology Evangelist and author of the blog www.miko.com*

"A concise and pleasurable read, *The Transformative Negotiator* takes the well-known basic tenets of negotiation and goes beyond to showcase the importance of *connection* in successful negotiations. Drawing on historical examples and her personal experience, Huff creates a book that, along with a sprinkling of realistic exercises throughout, will push your awareness of self and your ability to negotiate successfully to the next level."

—*Michael B. Horn*, *author,* Blended: Using Disruptive Innovation to Improve Schools, *Co-Founder and Executive Director, Education, Clayton Christensen Institute, named one of the 100 most important people in the advancement of the use of technology in education by* Tech & Learning *magazine*

The Transformative Negotiator

Negotiator

Changing The Way We Come to Agreement
from the Inside Out

Michèle Huff, J.D.

UNHOOKED BOOKS
an imprint of High Conflict Institute Press
Scottsdale, Arizona

Copyright © 2015 by Michèle Huff
Unhooked Books, LLC
7701 E. Indian School Rd., Ste. F
Scottsdale, AZ 85251
www.unhookedbooks.com

ISBN: 978-1-936268-80-1
eISBN: 978-1-936268- 81-8

Library of Congress Control Number: 2014952578

Cover and interior design by Jeff Fuller, Shelfish.weebly.com
Edited by Catherine Broberg
Cover painting by Natalie Goldberg

Printed in the United States of America

The publisher and author wish to thank Natalie Golberg for the donation of the cover painting titled The Great Tree (Banyan).

Author's photo (page 173) was provided courtesy of the University of New Mexico.

I dedicate this book to my father, Paul Huff, who started me in the deep end of the pool to teach me to be fearless, and to my grandmother, Berthe Baron, whose love and unconditional acceptance kept me afloat long after that first swim lesson.

Contents

ACKNOWLEDGMENTS

Creating this book required patience and perseverance. Like many lawyers, I love to write and secretly longed to be a published author. What I didn't realize was how much hard work was involved, or how lonely it would be. I owe a huge debt to those who contributed behind the scenes: my parents, who never stopped pushing me; the educators in high school, college, and law school who uncovered my "potential" and helped me live up to it; and the clients and negotiating partners who (unknowingly) provided lessons and stories for the book. I want to thank Natalie Goldberg, an amazing teacher who showed me how to reconnect my head, my heart, and my hand through writing practice. Thank you to Scott Edelstein, my editor, who took everything I knew about mindfulness and negotiation and helped me hone and polish it until it sparkled. To all the readers of my early manuscripts (friends and family, this is you), I appreciate your fresh eyes and helpful copyediting. A big thank you to Megan Hunter, my publisher at Unhooked Books, for believing in the power of transformation and to the team (editor Cathy Broberg, cover art designer Jeff Fuller, and many others) for their tireless efforts to make this book great. Thank you to my mother, Gisèle, an extraordinary woman who filled our New York City apartment with books and dissertation materials and encouraged me to pursue my passion for reading and learning. And to my loving partner, Terri, who nurtured me through the final stages of frantic rewrites and the agony of publishers' rejections. *Merci, mon étoile.*

Connection

Negotiation is the art of communicating with another person with the intent of modifying his or her behavior to satisfy your wants or needs.

Negotiation is a self-interested act: your goals are paramount. At the same time, it's a connected act, an act that requires cooperation from your negotiation partner, who also wants to satisfy his or her wants and needs. Coming to an agreement requires communication skills; preparedness; the proper use of intuition, leverage, and power; the ability to manage emotions; and most of all, patience and perseverance.

Negotiation is not the same as litigation, arbitration, or mediation. Those are third-party interventions in disputes. They are modes of *conflict resolution* that are used only after negotiations have stalled.

Negotiations are not limited to business transactions or court proceedings. We negotiate every day, in every aspect of our lives. You are negotiating when you ask your daughter to finish her homework, and when you demand a raise from your boss.

We negotiate for a variety of reasons: to motivate, to influence, to buy, to sell, or to solve a problem. Negotiations can be quite productive, or they can turn very sour. To successfully negotiate, we must be clear about our intent and mindful of the consequences of our behavior in coming to an agreement. This is just as true when you negotiate with your teenager about drug use as it was when George Mitchell brokered peace in Northern Ireland.

As you will discover in this book, negotiation isn't just about coming to a mutually acceptable agreement. It's also about being real, balanced, and vulnerable. Negotiation is *yin* and *yang;* it's about being complementary and interconnected. Like earth and sky, and light and dark, your interests and those of your negotiation partner are separate but intertwined.

I'm a technology and intellectual property lawyer, currently working for the University of New Mexico. I negotiate and solve problems for a living. I learned the basics of negotiation in law school and from reading classic texts, attending workshops, and practicing what I'd learned, both on and off the job.

But something always felt missing from the standard discourse and training in negotiation: *connection.* I found myself drawn to negotiation theories that contemplated more than just a party's bottom line or BATNA (best alternative to a negotiated agreement). I began to experiment by integrating elements from a wide range of wisdom, especially Buddhist teachings, into my negotiations to create a different kind of skill set. I then applied these skills to a variety of difficult situations, and they worked. Today I use them all the time.

I believe that my success as a negotiator has little to do with my lawyerly training or my use of logic and reason. Rather, I succeed in negotiations because I practice being mindful and in the moment, no matter how hard or painful that might be. I call this approach "transformative negotiation," because it moves parties past the mechanics of a transaction, beyond the two-dimensional win-win paradigm, and elevates the experience to a multidimensional interaction. Indeed, the power of transformative negotiation transcends the purely material aspects of a negotiation by tapping into its spiritual aspects, operating on a collective plane rather than an individual one. When you are empowered to negotiate this way, you suddenly view each interaction as an opportunity to transform yourself, your negotiation partner, and the world. Transformative negotiators balance wants and needs with the effects of materialism on human suffering, are driven less by self-interest and ego and more by empathy and compassion; they negotiate from the heart, not from the head.

I've written *The Transformative Negotiator* to help you use this method in your own negotiations. This is not a technical manual, but an honest, down-to-earth approach to negotiating and working with others. You will not see acronyms, graphs, or charts. Each short chapter draws on multiple disciplines to illustrate a concept, and includes examples from my own professional and personal life as well as from the lives of other successful negotiators. This book weaves together the spiritual and the strategic, emphasizing the soft skills that help us achieve realistic goals and positive outcomes.

As you will learn, this approach to negotiation is more holistic than linear, more of an art than a business. It is also profoundly effective and will change the way you interact with people in all areas of your life.

CHAPTER ONE

Really Listen

How often do you listen with your whole self when another person is speaking?

Listening requires full engagement, which is hard work. It takes stillness, patience, and time.

Some say that listening is a lost art, one that many people are starving for. Yet listening is not complicated.

To simply *listen* means to hold open a space (both around you and inside you) for what the other person is saying and feeling. It demands that you put down your iPad, smartphone, pen, or pencil, and focus your full attention on the speaker. It does not mean that you respond, offer a solution, or judge the content of what you hear in that moment.

Deep listening has both an active and a reflective component. The active portion requires you to concentrate on the speaker's words, feelings, and nonverbal cues, without filtering, responding, or judging. The reflective component requires you to move from listening to comprehension without engaging in censorship.

Active Listening

We usually hear what we want to hear, what we have been trained to hear, and nothing else. We focus on certain words or behaviors and ignore others. When we listen, we can be influenced by our own unique set of *filters* and *triggers*. Filters remove unpleasant or contentious content. Triggers precipitate actions, including behaviors—often unwanted ones.

In short, filters and triggers are pieces of baggage we all bring to the negotiating table. One of our tasks as transformative negotiators, then, is to identify that baggage and prevent it from blocking our ability to listen. We do this, in part, by naming it.

Let's consider Mario's triggers and filters. When Mario hears other people raise their voice, he tunes them out because yelling was how his father showed displeasure with Mario's behavior when he was young. Thus, a raised voice is a trigger for Mario that causes him not to hear subsequent communications. Mario also has a filter, based on his past experience, that people who raise their voice do so only to criticize him, not to emphatically make a point. In this case, both filter and trigger cause him to tune out the speaker.

Now let's look at another example. Janet, your employee, has a hard time hearing constructive criticism or, sometimes, comments of any kind about her work. When you start talking to Janet about her performance, you'll notice that she avoids eye contact and fidgets with her hands. If you ask whether she's heard what you've said, she may filter out any perceived negative elements in your question. Your attempt to probe further, to point out areas of concern, may trigger a defensive reaction, causing her to lash out at you.

While you are listening to someone like Mario or Janet,

note their behaviors and responses. But also watch for where you contract, so you can identify your own triggers and filters. Perhaps you feel inclined to respond aggressively to Janet's defensiveness. If so, catch yourself and try to stay open instead. Allow her to be defensive without getting redirected by your own trigger. This will not only make you a better listener; it might also break the cycle that occurs when you react to Janet with aggression and she, in turn, becomes even more defensive.

Listening and hearing are two different things. You can listen actively but still hear something other than what the speaker intended, because of your filters.

When Mario hears a raised voice, it may not matter that you're using words of praise to motivate him to apply to college. His filter may not allow him to take that message in. When you ask Janet to revise her work to conform to your department's standard format, she may only hear that her work is substandard, even if you begin the conversation by praising her skills. What's more, if her identity is wrapped up in her work, she may also take this feedback as a personal insult.

To be a transformative negotiator, you need to be alert to these triggers and filters, to recognize them when they appear, and to work around them to come to a mutually acceptable result. This might mean using a softer tone with Mario, or telling Janet that your requested revisions are stylistic, not substantive. (If their triggers and filters are deeply rooted, it may take you many attempts before they begin to mentally and emotionally rewire. That's okay. Be patient and persevere.)

Few people have been trained to really listen. Most of us, however, have learned how to defend ourselves against others, appear knowledgeable on all subjects of the negotiation (even those we may know little about), or act in a way that will make people like us. All of these can get in the way of a successful negotiation.

You know the situation. You've just explained a complex issue to a co-worker to get his buy-in to the project and he responds by telling you about a supposedly (but not actually) similar circumstance he encountered when he worked at that famous Wall Street firm. Maybe he doesn't even let you finish your explanation before he interrupts. And he won't hear what you're saying because he is so anxious to jump in with his own impressive story.

Rather than listening, we have learned to talk over the speaker or to focus on preparing responses in our heads. The more energy we spend doing this, the less energy we have to actively listen to what our negotiation partner says.

Cutting people off, offering advice, or providing a comparable story from your own life are not forms of listening.

Can you recall a time when you tried to be supportive of a friend, and failed? Perhaps they began with a tearful explanation of a recent crisis in their life, and you interrupted with a comment about a similar issue of your own. "Oh, that reminds me of the time when I . . ." With a deep sigh, they started over. This time, you cut them off with an idea for solving the problem. Finally, they screamed at you, "I just want you to listen, not give me advice!" Or maybe they just said "never mind" and changed the subject or ended the conversation.

Often the simple act of being heard is the ideal "solution" to a person's problem. And in negotiations, really hearing what the other person says may flip a switch that makes a resolution seem crystal clear.

Yet staying quiet is not easy for most of us. I used to be a terrible listener myself. In my professional life, people paid me to listen to their legal problems, quickly analyze the relevant issues, and come up with solutions. I was good at this and so enjoyed career success. But when I applied these same skills to my personal life, they didn't go over as well. I had to retrain my mind to stop analyzing and simply take in what my friends or loved ones were saying. I did this with slow breathing and many years of trial and error.

Active listening requires not immediately judging the content you hear. That's because the instant a judgment comes up, it blocks your listening. If you quickly articulate that judgment, it can also shut down your negotiation partner. So suspend your judgment and keep your mouth closed, at least for the moment.

Active listening also includes focusing not only on the words, but on the feelings and emotions behind the words as well. Pay attention to the tone, pitch, and volume of a person's voice. These can offer valuable clues about their feelings. Is their voice cracking? Do you notice a slight increase in volume or speed when they broach a certain topic? Is there a discrepancy between what the speaker says and how he or she says it? For example, does the person speak of relocating 1,000 employees in the same way you would describe removing a mound of earth from a construction site? Are they talking about the stock market dropping half a percentage point as if it were a terrorist attack? Nonverbal cues can be another way to help you assess the other person's emotional state. Is the speaker's posture open and receptive, or closed and defensive? (I'll talk more about posture in chapter 15.)

In any negotiation, the more open and receptive you are, the more likely you are to come to agreement—or to quickly discover that no agreement is possible.

Here's an exercise you can try to sharpen your active listening skills.

Try This:
Pick someone in your life—a friend or a co-worker—with whom you have trouble communicating and start a conversation with them. As they speak, focus on their words, tone, body language, and feelings. See if you can spot their triggers or filters. Maybe they seem challenged by your authority or want something from you that they can't articulate.

Listen more deeply still. Avoid the temptation to react or judge. At the same time, observe your own emotions. Are you angry? Frustrated? Impatient? What about your own filters or triggers—have they been activated by the conversation? Can you notice them, and then release their hold over you?

Practice talking with this person on a regular basis.

Reflective Listening

In negotiations, it is also important to clearly *understand* what the other person is saying, to be able to demonstrate that understanding, and to have that understanding verified (or, if necessary, corrected). This is known as reflective listening.

In his groundbreaking book *People Skills*, Dr. Robert Bolton provides a good definition of reflective listening:

The good listener responds reflectively to what the speaker is saying. She restates, in her own words,

the feeling and/or content that is being expressed—
and in doing so, communicates understanding and
acceptance. There are four basic reflecting skills.
Paraphrasing, the first of the reflective responses,
focuses on the speaker's *content*. The reflection of
feeling occurs when the listener concentrates on
feeling words, infers feelings from the general content,
"reads" body language, asks, "How would I feel if
I were doing or saying that?" and then mirrors the
feeling back to the speaker. The combined reflection of
feeling and content is called the reflection of *meaning*.
Summative reflections are very condensed recaps of
the most significant elements of a fairly long segment
of conversation.[1]

Reflective listening is not a simple technique you quickly
implement. It's a serious practice that requires your complete
and careful attention.

Paraphrasing content is an especially useful part of
reflective listening. It doesn't mean that you accept or agree
with the other person's position, but rather that you have
heard it accurately. And the more your negotiation partner
feels heard and understood, even if you respectfully disagree
with his or her position, the more open that person may be to
reaching an agreement with you. What's more, paraphrasing
what you've heard also helps *you* move closer to a correct
understanding.

In workplace mediations, I often ask one party to paraphrase
what the other person has said, but only after the speaker has
had his or her full say. For example, "Ted, did you hear what
Sally just said? She was explaining why she's upset with your
behavior. Can you repeat it back in your own words to let her

know that you've understood?"

Bolton's second response, *feeling*, increases your level of empathy for the other person. Developing awareness for the other person's feelings, putting yourself in his or her shoes, is especially important in dealing with conflict, which often arises during problematic negotiations. When you acknowledge that another person is angry (or hurt, or disappointed, or anything else), you go a long way toward creating a positive connection. Naming the feeling also helps to dispel and deflect its blocking energy.

When you are a listener, your job is to reflect both content and feeling back to your negotiation partner.

Let's look at how Bolton's reflective listening skills might help in a negotiation with your teenage son. You have asked him multiple times to clean up his room. Each time he refuses, and the room gets messier by the day. You're tired of the screaming matches that inevitably follow each request. So, this time, you practice reflective listening:

"Hal, will you please clean your room today?"

"No, I will not *please clean my room*—just like I've told you a hundred times already."

In a curious rather than angry tone—here's where controlling emotion comes into play—you ask, "Why are you giving me such a hard time about cleaning up your room?"

"It's my room and you should let me have it the way I want. It's none of your business!" His arms are crossed and voice is raised. You note the posture but don't judge or respond defensively.

"Okay, so I hear that you view my request as an invasion of your space and privacy. And you're angry about that. Is that right?"

Hal nods. "Duh, yeah, of course that's right."

"I respect your privacy, Hal. That's not what this is about. I don't need to come into your room or poke around in it. Do you think there might be another reason for my wanting you to clean your room?"

You have heard him and paraphrased his concern about privacy, and you have acknowledged his feelings—anger—in a nonconfrontational way. Hal's arms uncross and he leans forward. "What reason?"

"I need you to show me that you can take care of the things I've trusted you with. If you can't take care of your room, how will you be able to take care of a car when you're old enough to drive next year?"

Now you have confirmed Hal's position that his room is his domain but added a gentle reminder that the room is entrusted to him. You *didn't* say, "That's not your room; you're in my house and you'll do as I say!" Instead, you've shifted the focus away from an area that Hal doesn't care about (keeping his room clean) to one that he might care about a great deal (being permitted to drive a car). You've also reframed the entire discussion: it's now about your trust, not about violating his privacy. And you've created an opening for negotiation. (I'll show you how to reframe in chapter 12.)

You might then use *leverage* with Hal by offering him something he wants (a bigger allowance, computer time, music downloads, a later curfew) in return for cleaning his room. Or, perhaps, you offer to put $10 in an account toward buying his first used car every time he cleans his room. (I'll cover leverage in chapter 20.)

Another option is to ask Hal to reverse roles and have the

two of you paraphrase each other. Let him hear his reasons, and his attitude, coming out of your mouth. Then he can take your position, and your own attitude, and reflect them back to you. Here's how that exercise might sound.

You, acting as Hal: "Why can't you just leave me alone? You're always after me about something. If I want my room to be a pigsty, and smell like moldy gym shoes, it's none of your business."

Hal, acting as you: "It *is* my business, and what you want doesn't matter because you're just a teenager. I'm the boss around here and you'll do as I say. I'm the master and you're the servant."

This exchange might lead to a broader dialogue about Hal's feelings of being excessively monitored or of having no say in many decisions that concern him. That discussion might also focus on your job as a parent to set boundaries and your desire to not be questioned or resisted about every decision.

When you practice active and reflective listening, your partner in the negotiation is more likely to feel deeply heard. This encourages the negotiation to proceed in a positive way.

CHAPTER TWO

Say It Clearly, without Charge

Your overall goal in negotiating is to modify another's behavior to get what you want or need. To do this you must be able to clearly articulate what it is you want, need, and expect from your partner. It is your responsibility to create *clarity* by being specific and eliminating ambiguities.

When you ask your husband to get you chocolate at the grocery store, for example, he might buy a bag of peanut M&M's, a box of See's Candies, or a half-pound block of baker's chocolate. The word "chocolate" is open to interpretation. If you want a box of See's, ask for a box of See's. Even if your request for chocolate always means that you want See's, verify it. (Then, if one day you do just ask for some chocolate, your husband would be more likely to respond, "A box of See's, right?")

In this case you actually need to be even more specific, since See's comes in various sizes and combinations. Again, your responsibility as a negotiator is to drill down to exactly what you want and to make sure your negotiation partner understands.

Let's say what you're really craving is a large box of See's Nuts & Chews. Tell your husband this. Also give him a list of acceptable substitutes in order of priority. "If the store is out of Nuts & Chews, don't get anything. If they only have the small box, get that. Thanks."

In personal negotiations like this one, failing to be specific about your wants and needs may result in something like the wrong type of chocolate—in other words, the consequences are minimal, besides disappointing your sweet tooth. But other times, the consequences of ambiguity can have a much greater impact.

In more important business negotiations, parties who fail to remove ambiguities open themselves up to having a neutral third party—an arbitrator or judge—make the decision for them at a later date. Often that decision, made by a person not invested in the negotiations, results in an incorrect interpretation of your intent. This is not an enviable position for any negotiator, especially if the issue—duration, pricing, liability—is something you really care about. Don't stop negotiating until you've achieved a level of clarity that leaves no (or very little) room for interpretation.

What do I mean by room for interpretation? An example would be a contract to buy or sell goods that specifies payment in dollars. Does the term "dollars" refer to U.S. dollars, or Canadian, or Australian, or Zimbabwean? If you care about being paid in U.S. dollars, say so. Similarly, the word "includes" can be interpreted as a restrictive term (any item not on the list is excluded) or as an expansive term (items on the list are not exhaustive, but are provided simply as examples). If you want the list to be expansive, make sure you say "includes, but is not limited to, the following list."

At other times, ambiguity can arise from improper word placement. For example, if you say, "The artist will paint the model nude," we aren't clear whether the artist or the model will be disrobing for the project.

Negotiations are simple when your proposal requires a clear yes-or-no answer, or your negotiation partner has articulated clear and specific wants or needs. But when you don't have either of these, you must negotiate your way through the ambiguity. This usually involves asking clarifying questions until the waters run clear.

TRY THIS

The next time you negotiate something, make sure you've clearly articulated what you want and need. Check the other party's understanding, and ask the person to repeat these items back to you.

If necessary, repeat and clarify your wants and needs, being as specific as possible to remove any remaining ambiguities.

Then do the same in reverse. Say, "Here's my understanding of what you want and need . . . Is that correct?"

Repeat the process until both of you are satisfied that ambiguities have been removed and all gaps in understanding are closed.

Words can be positive, negative, or neutral. From an energy standpoint, they can also be emotionally flat or emotionally charged. In negotiations, it's almost always best to use neutral words that are emotionally flat.

In Buddhism, this principle is embodied in one factor of the Noble Eightfold Path, called Right Speech (the other seven are Right View, Right Thought, Right Action, Right Livelihood, Right Effort, Right Mindfulness, and Right Concentration). In his book *Mindfulness: A Practical Guide to Awakening*, teacher Joseph Goldstein explains that this factor "is such a powerful influence in our lives because we speak a lot." True, especially, for lawyers and negotiators. Goldstein goes on to say, "Speech conditions our relationships, conditions our minds and hearts, and conditions karmic consequences in the future."[2] The other aspects of Right Speech include truthfulness, refraining from gossip or slander, refraining from useless or frivolous talk, and the topic we covered in the last chapter, mindful listening. The aspect we're dealing with now is emotional tone, or being conscious of the energy behind our word choices.

There are exceptions to the rule stated above, however, times when the use of a positive, emotionally charged word or phrase might be appropriate. I'm thinking of the annual performance review where an employee hears (hopefully not for the first time) what he or she has been doing to meet or exceed your expectations, and is enthusiastically encouraged to do more of the same.

What do I mean by words having a charge? As an example, let's consider several ways to describe a person's left-leaning political viewpoint: We could use the positive word "progressive," which is emotionally flat; the neutral term "liberal," which is emotionally charged; or the negative "ssocialist"—or, worse, the derogatory "pinko"—which are both emotionally charged.

It's easy to see how the use of positive and emotionally flat terms would be accepted into the conversation with ease, while the negative and emotionally charged terms may incite strong reactions that take away from the actual work of the negotiation.

Don't forget that, even if you consciously select neutral, emotionally flat words, or even positive ones, your negotiation partner may have personal filters or triggers through which he or she translates your words.

Imagine a negotiation between two co-workers, Eileen and Blake. Blake has delegated tasks to Eileen, and she has willingly accepted those tasks. But Eileen is now angry with Blake. She spends fifteen minutes telling Blake in detail the myriad ways in which he jumped into her work and then undermined her with higher-ups. She is quite specific, referring to notes she took at the time of each incident. When she is done, she looks at Blake for a response.

Blake says quietly, "None of that ever happened. You're a filthy liar."

It's hard to get a sense from ink on paper, but these last words might have been spoken in a flat tone or an angry one. In this case, Blake's affect was flat, not angry, but nonetheless, his selection was ill-advised.

Eileen's eyes narrow, but instead of escalating the conflict and calling him a bastard, she stops herself and uses reflective listening. "So, Blake, what I hear you saying is that I concocted every one of these incidents. They never happened. Is that right?"

Blake pauses. "Well, no . . . In a sense they all took place. But you've highly exaggerated the facts."

Eileen nods and says, "Thanks, Blake. So it sounds like you agree with me that the events took place, but you're saying that

I've twisted or misrepresented most of the details. Am I hearing you correctly?"

Blake sighs. "No, you're not. I'm not saying that you're deliberately twisting the facts. I'm saying that you're not interpreting them correctly. You're misunderstanding my intentions. I'm not trying to sabotage you. I'm just trying to move the work forward."

This statement is quite a bit different from "You're a filthy liar." Now the negotiations have the potential to proceed in a positive way.

Using neutral words and charge-free language in negotiations is just as important as being clear and specific in your speech and listening deeply. Choose your words wisely.

CHAPTER THREE

Check Assumptions and Expectations

A s we've seen in the previous two chapters, successful negotiation depends on the quality of people's listening and speech. But as speakers, we have one additional task. We need to be aware of how—and whether—our message is being received. Each time we speak, even if we do so with clarity and neutrality, our meaning or intention may still be misinterpreted by listeners based on their *assumptions* and *expectations* (as well as on their filters and triggers).

In practice, speaking and listening are inextricably linked in a continuous flow. In her book *That's Not What I Meant! How Conversational Style Makes or Breaks Relationships,* Dr. Deborah Tannen explains this phenomenon:

> At any point, each person is both reacting to and causing a reaction in others. Most of us tend to see ourselves as responding to what others say, without

realizing that what they are saying may be a reaction to us. *Communication is a continuous stream* in which everything is simultaneously a reaction and an instigation, an instigation and a reaction.[3] (emphasis mine)

We've already talked about how filters and triggers can block the listening flow of a communication stream. Now we'll look at how assumptions and expectations can arise at any (or every) stage of a negotiation and cause gaps in that flow.

If our negotiation partner has a certain way of posing or responding to a question, we might make an incorrect assumption about the person's intent, or have an unrealistic expectation about how the negotiation will proceed. Here's an example:

Maya asks her husband, Peter, "Where should we go for dinner?" Peter immediately names a local restaurant he likes. Maya finishes getting dressed but doesn't respond to Peter's suggestion. He drives to the restaurant, they eat, and the food is terrible. As they leave, Maya says, "I didn't want to go here in the first place."

Peter responds, "Why didn't you say something?"

She says, "Because you had your mind made up to come here. Besides, you don't care about my opinion; you always do what you want."

Let's dissect each spouse's contribution to this conflict, paying careful attention to their assumptions and expectations.

When Maya asked, "Where should we go for dinner?" she wasn't expecting her husband to name a specific restaurant; she really wanted to discuss what kind of fare each of them was in the mood for. In this case, Maya failed in her responsibility as a negotiator to be clear and to mean what she said. To get the results she was after, she might have said, "I'm in the mood for Italian. Which restaurant should we choose tonight?" Or better still, she could have engaged Peter with, "I'm in the mood for Italian, Peter; what about you?" If she did want to go to a specific place, she could have said, "I'd like to go to Andiamo tonight. Are you okay with that?" Or, if she really didn't have any preference about the type of food they ate, or if she wanted to solicit Peter's input without having a particular restaurant in mind, she could have simply said, "I'm not sure what I'm in the mood for; what about you, Peter?"

So that's the first gap in the communication flow—between what Maya said and what she meant to say.

There might also have been varying *expectations* about how negotiations could best proceed. Maya likes to start negotiations with a somewhat vague or abstract request and then move to specificity in a back-and-forth dialogue. Peter prefers to offer a specific proposal and negotiate from there. (Such differences can be based on culture, gender, generation, or even all three.) In Peter and Maya's case, Peter inadvertently hijacked the negotiation by simply suggesting a specific restaurant. He made an *assumption*, based on Maya's question, that she was inviting him to suggest a specific restaurant. And so Peter's response was to choose a restaurant because he believed Maya wanted him to decide where they would dine that evening: "Let's go to the Owl." He also assumed that Maya would object if she didn't like his choice.

Instead, Peter might have checked out his assumption by asking Maya, "Do you want me to decide or to make a suggestion?"

If Peter did have a specific restaurant or type of food in mind, he might have said, "I'm craving American food. How about the Owl?" Maya might then have sensed an opening and said, "I'm fine with American, but not the Owl. I went there for lunch last week and it was awful."

Here's the next gap. After Peter heard a request for specificity, not for a suggestion, he made an assumption— perhaps based on his experience of the way these conversations usually go—that Maya didn't really care where they had dinner. Or by naming a specific restaurant, he might have intended to offer a proposal for Maya to respond to. But that's not what he said, and it's certainly not what Maya heard.

What Maya did hear Peter do was make a decision that she interpreted as non-negotiable. For Maya, the specificity of Peter's response was a trigger that shut down the negotiations for her. Rather than rejecting the restaurant Peter suggested, or offering her own opinion or a counter-proposal, she stayed quiet. The dining disaster might have been avoided if Maya had simply spoken up and said, "You know, I had lunch there and the food wasn't good."

If I could counsel Peter on his communication style, I would advise him to listen more actively, especially to nonverbal cues. What was Maya's demeanor? Was she upset? What, if anything, did she express after he mentioned the Owl? Why did he interpret her silence as agreement?

Using reflective listening, Peter might also have said, "Is the Owl okay, or would you prefer somewhere else for dinner?" Or, "Honey, you're not talking. Is something wrong?" Assuming Maya would honestly respond to these cues instead of staying quiet, the dining disaster might have been easily averted—all because of a few mindful words on Peter's part.

The transformative negotiator must be aware of potential disruptions in the flow of a negotiation and address them by checking out assumptions and expectations. This can move both parties closer to mutual understanding and, ultimately, agreement.

CHAPTER FOUR

Know Thyself— and Much More

Every successful negotiation requires that from the outset you know yourself and, as much as possible, know your negotiation partner. You can never be too prepared for a negotiation—and you can all too easily be unprepared.

You should also try to learn as much as you can about the specific circumstances surrounding the negotiation.

Here are two common examples:

If you're conducting a job search, read each prospective employer's latest annual report; talk to current and past employees; and research comparable salaries and benefits for the position. Also, try to determine whether it is a new position or one that was previously occupied—and, if the latter, why did the person leave? If external issues (such as the company's record on the environment or its philanthropic activities) are important to you, dig deeper to unearth them. In interviews, ask clear, specific questions about anything that's pertinent to your decision. Make sure you understand not only what will be expected of you and how your potential boss defines success, but what the company expects to achieve in the next five years and how *it* defines success. Imagine the toughest questions that the employer may ask you, and decide on and rehearse your responses ahead of time.

If you're looking for a doctor, lawyer, accountant, real estate agent, or another professional you intend to put your trust in, always interview them before signing on. In addition, insist on references, and be wary if someone refuses; it may signal that they don't have satisfied clients. Lawyers, doctors, and financial advisors are licensed by legal, medical, and financial organizations; check those organizations for disciplinary actions. Also check the Better Business Bureau for complaints. Find out how independent rating agencies (Consumer Reports, Angie's List, and so on) rate a product, service, or company. The Internet makes these inquiries easy. You don't even need to own a computer; just go to the public library.

Never allow yourself to be pressured into a decision. Always get the facts, consider them carefully, and then make a decision when you are ready.

When you begin any negotiation, find out who has authority to close the deal. This can be a relatively simple task, or it may be a constantly moving target. Whoever has that authority at the beginning of a negotiation might not maintain it; your job is to continually probe, and adjust as necessary.

For example, think of a time when you were negotiating over the phone with a company representative for a credit to your account. After a while, you found yourself saying, "Let me speak to your supervisor," because you realized that the person on the other end didn't have the authority to give you what you needed. Or perhaps the representative said, "For that I'll have to transfer you to our dispute resolution department. Please hold."

As much as possible, try to negotiate directly with the person or people who have the power to make a decision—or, at the very least, are closely connected to the decision maker(s) and can recommend a decision.

Also discuss up front any details about how a decision will be made and approved. For example, at the state university where I work, an executive may have signature authority according to our business policy, but the deal still has to be approved by our seven-member Board of Regents—or even, in some cases, by a separate state entity such as the Department of Higher Education.

Early on in any negotiation, let your negotiation partner know your own chain of authority. For example, during lawyer-to-lawyer negotiations, it is common for each lawyer to give advice to their respective decision-maker clients but not to carry responsibility for making the actual decision.

Cultural differences may be a factor here. For instance, Native American tribes typically make decisions communally, in a tribal council. Similarly, in some large organizations—county governments and movie studios, for instance—layers of approvals may be required for many important decisions. Knowing the decision-making process ahead of time will help you to work within the system instead of fighting it. We will address these issues in more detail in chapter 8.

You might also ask your negotiation partner to tell you a bit about the decision-maker(s), their past decisions, how they might view the deal you're working on, or what might make them disapprove its terms.

If the approval process will be cumbersome, plan for the additional time required to have the negotiation approved. This will help you avoid being frustrated by the inevitable delays.

Know Yourself

On a blank piece of paper, and without stopping to think, take a minute or two to write a laundry list of your personal characteristics. These should be adjectives and nouns that describe you as a person. Be gentle, but realistic. Don't limit yourself to the negotiation arena; include all facets of your life.

Then take another few minutes to separate the items on this list into three categories: strengths, weaknesses, and neutral characteristics.

Now, look at how you classified your strengths and weaknesses. We associate strengths with a positive value, and weaknesses with a negative one. But every attribute can be calibrated depending on context and circumstance. A word or phrase in the positive column could easily migrate to the negative one under certain conditions, and vice versa. For example, if "prone to compromise" appears in your weakness column, it might just as easily go into your strength column as "flexibility."

The point here is not what you've written on your list. What's important is that you honestly accept what you've written about yourself and that you see how each item can be used in a positive or negative way, regardless of the category you placed it in.

Bruce Lee, the Chinese martial artist, was nearsighted and his right leg was one inch shorter than his left. But he managed to transform these "shortcomings" into potent weapons; he would lead from his left and draw his sparring partners close in. By accepting and adjusting in this way, he became one of the greatest fighters of all time. He founded his own martial arts system, Jeet Kune Do, with a philosophy of "using no way as way and having no limitation as limitation."

One of my own attributes is that I tend to speak loudly and authoritatively. Sometimes this may come across to my negotiation partner as opinionated, strong-willed, or even intractable. I have learned to adapt my natural style so that I project confidence without overstepping others' boundaries. Put another way, I try to be assertive without becoming aggressive. What's the difference? Assertive: inclined to bold assertion; confident. Aggressive: inclined to move or act in a hostile fashion. The stance I assume is confident, not hostile. I learned to do this by adjusting my voice, actively listening, pausing to allow my partner to respond, and remembering to breathe.

We must each identify our attributes and inclinations as negotiators, and then adapt them to be as useful as possible.

Know Your Negotiation Partner

How do you learn about your negotiation partner? Observation is one way. Research is another. A third is asking direct questions. This assumes, of course, that you can trust what your partner tells you. (Research and observation will usually tell you how trustworthy they are.)

Let's use the job search example I mentioned earlier to flesh this out. When you did your homework to learn everything you could about the company/employer, did you find out who the hiring manager is? Assume you did. Who is this person? Do you know anyone in your network (professional, academic) who might know him or her? Employees either currently at the company or who have recently left? How long has the job posting been active? Has there been turnover in the department, and if so, can you find out why?

When I negotiate as a lawyer, it helps me to know how my negotiation partner views my role. Many see lawyers as roadblocks, trained to eliminate risk and say no. Through that lens, my proposals may be viewed as tiresome legalistic maneuvers that prevent my partners from reaching their ultimate goal. So, early in the negotiation, I try to help my negotiation partners see me as a creative facilitator instead of as someone determined to get in their way.

The more information the you and your negotiation partner have about each other—regardless of how it is obtained— the more likely you both are to negotiate from a place of understanding instead of misunderstanding.

In most situations, you will negotiate for yourself one-on-one with a negotiation partner. Sometimes, however, you may negotiate for someone else or even represent multiple parties.

When you negotiate on someone else's behalf, you are trying to modify your negotiation partner's behavior to satisfy your client's or employer's wants and needs. In this case, it's important to regularly check in with your employer or client throughout the negotiation to make sure you are accurately expressing the party's intent and working to achieve the correct goals.

If you're negotiating on behalf of multiple parties, make sure you get buy-in from *everyone* you represent before you take a position that binds the entire group. This is rarely easy. Often conflicting preferences and priorities arise, with each party arguing for a different point of view. You'll need to take the time and trouble to build consensus. Managing these group interactions is part of your role as a transformative negotiator. Typically, you will find yourself facilitating a separate negotiation among all the parties you represent. The techniques in this book can, of course, be used in these side negotiations as well. For instance, if one issue is particularly thorny, leave it until the end; give the people you represent time to agree on other issues and begin to trust each other. Only then, once trust has been established and other agreements have been worked out, should you tackle the toughest issues.

Collective bargaining negotiations present unique multiparty opportunities, as you will see from this next vignette.

In 1987, the National Football League had twenty-eight teams; a player representative for each team who handled union matters with individual players; a policy-making board for the players; and a management council for the league. In negotiations regarding the issue of free agency, the challenge was to satisfy these divergent interests while maintaining solidarity among the respective parties.

Players wanted to *maximize income during their short careers* and the *flexibility to change teams.*

Owners wanted *to control players' salaries* and *to maintain team stability.*

The parties mediated the dispute but, ultimately, the union rejected the owners' proposal and voted to strike.

The NFL was prepared; it immediately hired lesser qualified replacements and kept playing football games. The union was unprepared; it hadn't built up a strike fund to provide its members with financial support and so quickly began running out of money. As players forfeited more of their pay, solidarity within the union began to crack. By week three, about 15 percent of the regular players had broken ranks and gone back to work. The union no longer spoke for the players, and the strike failed.

If you are negotiating for various parties, you likely have buy-in from them all at the outset of the negotiations, but you have to remain vigilant and make sure you continue to speak for them with one unified voice. This means communicating clearly and regularly with all parties, holding alliances of sometimes-contentious parties together, and adapting as circumstances change.

Preparedness in negotiations is one of the transformative negotiator's many tools, but in my view, it's the most critical one.

CHAPTER FIVE

Ask Why You Are Negotiating

Another essential component of being prepared in negotiations is to understand your purpose and your negotiation partner's purpose. What is motivating the negotiation? The best way to do this is to ask why you are negotiating and to be clear about your ultimate goals, and then to ask the same of your partner.

Start off with each party drafting a statement of purpose—the why of the negotiation. In traditional negotiation theory, *position* is what you say you want; *interest* is what you need and why you need it, plus what you want and why you want it. Position-based negotiation often fails because your partner doesn't understand why you want or need something. Interest-based negotiation is typically more successful because both sides begin the negotiation with at least a partial understanding of each other.

A statement of purpose is a high-level summary of what each of you expects from the negotiation. You might prepare one in advance, send it to your partner before your negotiation begins, and ask for one in return. Usually, if you ask, you'll get it. This will help focus the negotiation and smooth the way forward.

If you don't receive a statement from your partner, you might then legitimately wonder whether the person is withholding something from you. In this case, proceed with caution. It's also possible, though rare, that your negotiating partner will send you a deliberately misleading statement of purpose. This won't become clear until well into the negotiations, of course. In both such cases, you have good reason to doubt the trustworthiness of your negotiation partner and you must decide whether it is worth proceeding with the negotiation. You might want to confront your partner directly or try to discover his or her true purpose on your own. Be mindful of the fact that trust is like a delicate flower that must be nurtured, as we'll explore in chapter 18.

Being honest about purpose is not the same as giving away your game plan. It's the "why" of the negotiation, not the "how." Some examples of purpose:

- To obtain the license to publish your book in French for a reasonable price, but the lowest price possible
- To sell the license to publish that book for a fair price, but at the highest price possible

Keep in mind that any statement of purpose is merely a draft, not a straitjacket. It can be amended as needed as the negotiation progresses. Don't become too fixated on words that have been committed to paper. Stay focused on the flow of the negotiation.

TRY THIS

Think of an upcoming business negotiation (or a past one), and write out a purpose statement for it. This should be concise, perhaps a paragraph long. It should set forth what you hope to receive from the negotiation; it should also explain why you want that outcome.

Now write it from your negotiation partner's point of view. What does my partner want or need, why, and can I offer it? This will provide insight into how your partner will view your purpose and help you craft one that speaks to his or her needs.

In the job interview, your purpose may be to get the job, but it's also to give the employer a reason to hire you.

When you're done, look both statements over. Have you been fully honest and clear about your purpose, and done your best to understand your partner's? If not, rewrite it until you are.

"Why?" has become an increasingly important question to ask. In his book *Start with Why: How Great Leaders Inspire Everyone to Take Action*, Simon Sinek makes the case for continually examining and re-examining the why, the purpose for your life, work, and relationships. Although his focus is on leaders who inspire loyalty—and enjoy success—by articulating their own life purposes, the same lessons can be applied to transformative negotiation. Know the why and you will be much more likely to succeed in satisfying wants and needs—yours *and* your negotiation partner's.

Let's walk through a negotiation between two technology companies that quickly deteriorates because the negotiating partners aren't clear with each other about why they are negotiating.

NewCo develops software called ProTo that makes electronic devices interactive. GameCo is a manufacturer of a video game box similar to Xbox. NewCo, a start-up, is anxious to land its first customer and show a return on its investment; GameCo, an established company, needs a leg up on its highly successful Japanese rivals, Nintendo and Sega. The deal is potentially lucrative for both parties.

NewCo wants to grant a nonexclusive license, limit modifications to the software, and get paid a fee for every device sold. GameCo wants to lock in exclusivity, be allowed to modify the software, and pay a single licensing fee to avoid eating into its sensitive price margins.

The two firms begin negotiating. However, all that GameCo tells NewCo is that it wants to use NewCo's software at a reasonable price.

For three and a half months, the negotiations go nowhere. Eventually, the two CEOs call a summit. Only then do they discover each other's real purpose:

- NewCo: *To license ProTo to run on many different hardware platforms, at a fair royalty, while maintaining strict control of the programming interface.*
- GameCo: *To license interactive technology in a proprietary game cartridge on an exclusive basis or else buy out that technology.*

Had the parties revealed up front why they were negotiating and what they really wanted, the negotiations would have been much more productive and much less difficult. For example, NewCo could have offered GameCo a time-to-market window that satisfied its need to stay ahead of the competition as well as some degree of freedom to make modifications. At worst, it would have quickly become apparent to both companies that a deal was not possible.

Using a statement of purpose enhances the chance of success and avoids wasting time on negotiations that are doomed to fail.

CHAPTER SIX

Create Optimal Conditions

Where and when you negotiate can be as important as how and why.

First, the *where*:

Some negotiators will try to gain the upper hand by manipulating the physical energy of a room (temperature, light, seating arrangements) or the pacing of the negotiation (when to start, end, and break). Staying awake to these manipulations, adjusting to them, and using the anchors we'll discuss in chapter 16, will increase the likelihood that these techniques will have little or no effect on you.

You're familiar with most formal negotiation settings. When you haven't been able to secure a neutral spot, you might find yourself in a lawyer's conference room, or in the principal's office, or at a diplomatic table. Parties sit across from each other, literally taking sides.

But when the negotiating space creates sides, it also tends to create rigidity and an all-or-nothing model, with winners and losers. Even in the case of win-win negotiating strategies, negotiators who sit opposite each other start off by emphasizing the gulf between them, rather than by acknowledging how they're connected and how their divergent positions are also interrelated.

Given the chance, I never sit with members of my own negotiating team. I either sit with the other side or in a neutral spot. When I can arrange the room, I set up a round table, which of course has no sides.

Facing a window during a negotiation is supposed to put you at a disadvantage because your mind may be distracted by the view. I have found just the opposite to be true. When I negotiate, my analytical brain goes into overdrive, which means I can lose my connection to intuition and creativity. Staring at the sky or the tops of trees activates my creative, intuitive mind. This helps to create a more balanced way of seeing, thinking, and feeling. My mental view broadens with my physical view.

In informal negotiations, try to find a quiet place, somewhere with limited distractions. The living room in your house (if it's like mine, with an HDTV and stereo) is not a great place, but perhaps the porch or patio is.

Next, the *when*:

Part of knowing yourself is knowing your optimal time to negotiate. My mind is clearest at the start of each day, so that is when I try to schedule all negotiations. When the sun goes down, I move into *yin* time, which for me means relaxation and, ultimately, sleep. My patience is also usually low at this time. So I avoid scheduling negotiations near the end of the day or late at night.

Hormones may affect negotiations. I recently attended a conference on the neuroscience of mediation. What I learned was that all stress-response hormones are not alike. Some (like cortisol) flood the system and stay in the body for longer periods of time, while others (such as adrenaline) come and go quickly. Estrogen rushes and high testosterone levels, which in younger men peak in the morning and gradually lessen throughout the day, can make it more difficult to come to agreement. Science dictates that we schedule times of lower emotion/stress/hormones to enhance the flow of negotiations.

If I can't control when the negotiation will happen, I try to rest and get fully oxygenated before the session, either through a brisk walk or some form of cardio exercise. If a negotiation spills over into the evening hours, I've learned how to take care of myself, physically and mentally, so that I don't get swept away by the pressures of a harsh external environment and a mind that longs to tune out.

The timing of a negotiation is also important in terms of the cycle or unfolding of events. We've heard a lot about the best times of the year to buy a car or to put your house on the market. Similarly, good negotiators are strategic about when they choose to negotiate and when they choose to wait.

In early 2002, Disney's CEO Michael Eisner reviewed a rough cut of the movie *Finding Nemo* by Pixar and was underwhelmed. Disney and Pixar were partners under the terms of a distribution agreement that was up for renewal, but the relationship between Eisner and Steve Jobs, then Pixar's CEO, had become contentious. Eisner convinced the Disney board that they should wait to renegotiate the distribution agreement with Pixar. He predicted Pixar's creative failure with *Nemo*, which would give Disney better leverage over the terms of the deal.

Meanwhile, up the road, the Pixar design team also knew they had a loser in *Nemo*, so they worked tirelessly to revise everything about the film from the ground up. But Eisner and

Disney were unaware of the intensive work going on in the Northern California studio.

The reworked movie was a huge success, winning the 2003 Academy Award for best animated feature film. Disney paid dearly for putting off a new deal, losing rather than gaining leverage in negotiating the next distribution agreement.[4]

Now let's turn the tables. What if Disney had offered to renew the distribution agreement before *Nemo* hit theaters, and Pixar had agreed? Or what if Pixar's creative team hadn't been able to improve the picture, as Eisner predicted? Then Pixar wouldn't have been able to leverage the blockbuster's significant momentum, and monetary success, into a better deal with Disney.

Athletes want to renegotiate contracts after the regular season, but before the end of the postseason. Publishers want to negotiate the terms for a second book before the first one is finished. Everyone takes risks in negotiations. Your job as a negotiator is to find out what, if any, external timing factors may be at play. The timing of a negotiation is not always something you can control, but it helps to be as prepared and aware of potential consequences as possible.

Your job is to also know *when* to walk away from a negotiation. Sometimes the energetics are not working, or the relationships are not aligned. Or, as you get closer to the end of negotiations, you may sense that the outcomes will not be optimal.

Being able to say "no" in a negotiation isn't easy, but it is a very liberating practice. Being able to hear "no" also has positive consequences. It is a critical element of the principle of non-attachment, one of the aspects of practicing mindfulness.

One criticism of Harvard Business School's traditional "Getting to Yes" negotiation model is that it can result in short-circuiting the process and ultimately making sacrifices that are not in the best interests of either party. "Yes" is an end point in these negotiations, whereas "no" is a beginning. This is the premise of Jim Camp's book *Start with No . . . The Negotiating Tools That the Pros Don't Want You to Know,* filled with stories about how unleashing the "no" produced positive results. His style has been called militaristic, but many of the coaching principles he teaches negotiators at his boot camps mirror ones I cover from a softer, more spiritual perspective. One such element is the wisdom of "no" in helping us choose between what is skillful and what is not, what brings us true happiness and what causes only suffering. Saying "no" is the ultimate act of letting go.

Try This:

Think about the last negotiation you had and write out your purpose statement with invitations to say and hear "no." For example:

I would like this opportunity, but if I'm not the right person for the job, please let me know so that I can consider other options.

Your publishing house is one of my top choices, but if my manuscript isn't a good fit, I'll move on to my next choice.

We want to license our technology to you, but we may not be the right partner for your needs, and it might not make business sense to do a deal.

Notice how starting from this place opens up the possibilities, both from your standpoint (you are not afraid of "no"; you have options) and from your partner's ("This person cares about my needs; I want to work with them.").

When I had my own law practice, a client came to me in crisis. His start-up company was going through a forced merger, a consequence of the events of 9/11. Several years earlier, he had negotiated an employment contract which provided that if his job became obsolete as a result of a merger (or the removal of the CEO), he would be paid a year's salary. These severance protections were (and are) fairly common in his industry. The problem was that the company's board of directors had not approved the terms of *this* particular severance deal.

My client was adamant that he and the CEO had negotiated his employment terms in good faith, yet something nagged at his conscience—the board had been kept in the dark, which he was unaware of at the time he signed.

The board was furious with the CEO for not disclosing the severance until the last minute. But they needed to resolve the issue quickly to salvage any chance they might have to merge the faltering start-up. Here's what my client heard:

"You don't want to take the full severance. It will cripple the new venture and we're already handicapped."

"You're not entitled to a severance because you negotiated that deal in bad faith, without board approval."

"We'll sue you to void the deal."

My client knew that the board couldn't afford a lawsuit, that their threat was probably a bluff. But he didn't want to stick around to find out. He countered with half the severance amount, payable in a lump sum instead of over six months, and his offer was accepted.

Could my client have insisted on the plain terms of the contract, being paid one year's salary? Yes, of course. Could I guarantee him that the board would not sue to void the contract?

No, I could not. Was he right to walk away from the original deal rather than fight for it? Yes, because he had determined that to stay the course might cause him financial, emotional, and reputational harm. He did not get what he contracted for in the original negotiation, but he realized that money and fairness were no longer his only (or even primary) considerations; instead, his overriding need was to avoid litigation, which he did. (This is also a good example of understanding true need, as we'll learn more about in chapter 11.)

Here's another story of a negotiator walking away from a negotiation:

Jon M. Hunstman, CEO and chief negotiator for the Huntsman Corporation, and author of *Winners Never Cheat: Everyday Values We Learned as Children (But May Have Forgotten)*, tells the story of how he worked to negotiate Hunstman Chemical's acquisition of Sweetheart Plastics. Sweetheart was represented by an aggressive New York investment-banking firm. After protracted negotiations that lasted several months, Huntsman, with hard-fought financing in hand, made his final offer of $800 million, an upper limit the parties had discussed throughout the negotiations.

The bankers came back that same day with a take-it-or-leave-it $900 million bottom line, claiming they had other offers on the table. Huntsman, who did not know whether it was a bluff, a lie, or the truth, was very upset and called a several-hour negotiation time-out. (A time-out can be useful when you need to adjust your posture [chapter 15], pause to allow time for comprehension [chapter 16], or gain control of your emotions [chapter 23].)

When he returned at midnight, Huntsman insisted that he

would not pay a penny over $800 million, and then he walked away. It might have been that he didn't have access to other financing sources and couldn't raise any more money for the deal. It might also have been that he was so disgusted with the bankers' behavior that he didn't want to do business with them.

In either case, Sweetheart did not accept his final offer and took the next-highest offer, which came in at $660 million from a firm that "neither knew how to operate the business nor had put together the proper financial package."[5] Sweetheart did not fare well in the deal. The company lost $140 million and bought itself a lawsuit for unethical behavior; then, two years later, it sold again for $445 million, roughly half of Huntsman's original offer.

Sometimes what you believe to be the desired end point may not turn out to be the end at all—nor will it even prove desirable. This is especially true when you're negotiating for money. Your job as a transformative negotiator is to see past the presumed end point into empty space and stay awake to the shifting dynamics of the negotiation.

CHAPTER SEVEN

Do It in Person

When possible and practical, negotiate in person. Much of human communication involves facial expression, body language, gestures, and other visual clues. The fewer of these you have to read, the more difficult a negotiation can become. Negotiating in person also gives you the opportunity to connect with your partner in ways that help you get to know him or her better, something we've covered in previous chapters.

When you can't negotiate in person, a teleconference is your second-best option. If using Skype or some other video-conferencing tool is impossible, however, use the phone. Email provides the least information and the fewest nuances; use it only when you genuinely have to or to handle inconsequential matters or tie up loose ends.

Some other observations about phone and email negotiations:

Sometimes people try to accomplish other tasks when

they're on the phone. (And, more and more, this happens during face-to-face negotiations as well, when people repeatedly check or otherwise use their smartphones or tablets.) Negotiating always requires your full, focused attention. Don't multitask during a negotiation, and don't let your negotiation partner do it either. If you sense that there are others in the room with them making demands, or if you can hear them typing while they talk to you and the typing doesn't involve taking notes or revising a document, suggest finding another time to negotiate. You can say something like this: "It's important to me that we both focus on this discussion. If you're not able to do that right now, let's set up a time when we're both free to talk without distractions."

Because visual clues are not available to you in phone negotiations, pay extra attention to how something is said and to how your own words are received. Make sure you remember to employ your active and reflective listening skills. If you are on a conference call with many other people in a room and several others on the phone, observe all the rules of etiquette that you would when negotiating in person. Take the time to identify everyone in the room for the people on the phone, and make sure each caller is identified, can hear, and be heard. During the conversation, make sure everyone is allowed to have their say. This can be challenging during phone negotiations. When you can't observe the cues that indicate when a person is finished speaking, it's easy to interrupt or talk over each other.

As far as email is concerned, its biggest limitation is that it's one-dimensional. Negotiators often think they're thoroughly explaining what they need, but huge chunks of information may get omitted. Tone doesn't come across well in email, except for ALL CAPS that usually indicate anger. Moreover, there's no immediate give-and-take.

One benefit of email is that you have an opportunity to revise your words to get them right. You can review what you've written, eliminate ambiguity, and make sure you've included all the relevant information. Only then should you press the "send" button.

Caution: Never send any email in the heat of high emotion. Write it, rewrite it, save it, walk away, and review it a few hours (or days) later. If you still feel it reflects what you want to say and the way you want to say it, have someone else review it before it goes out.

When you receive information via email, remember to apply the same reflective listening techniques to the content as if your negotiation partner were sitting next to you. For example, I find it useful to read the message out loud to ensure that it makes sense. People use shorthand and incomplete sentences in emails. If there is ambiguity, send a reply email summarizing your understanding of their negotiation position and requesting further clarification of the points that are unclear, just the way you learned in chapter 2.

CHAPTER EIGHT

Consider Language and Culture

Up until now, my stories and examples have involved people who speak the same language. But what happens when you negotiate with someone whose native language is different from yours? Or, what if you and your negotiation partner speak a common language but don't operate within the same cultural framework?

Linguistic structures—the relationship of words in a sentence—can vary significantly from one language to another. English uses a subject-verb-object model. But not every language follows that configuration. Japanese, for example, follows a subject-object-verb model. In many languages multiple words are used to describe a single thing. The list of linguistic permutations is endless.

Negotiating with a Japanese partner vividly illustrated

this for me. Besides differences in sentence structure, his style of speech wasn't similar to mine. Instead of confronting the subject or speaking directly, he would hedge or subtly work his way around to the subject in slow motion. Meaning was often implicit rather than explicit. Michihiro Matsumoto, a writer on Japanese negotiation, sums up the approach in this way: "The United States is a *why-because* culture. Japan is a *non-why, non-because* culture" (emphasis mine).[6]

I learned by reading Matsumoto's book and others that my Japanese partner's "no" rarely meant "no," and I had to ask for something three times before he was prepared to take it seriously. Moreover, his statements, as a reflection of his linguistic and cultural rules, tended to be "we" oriented, while mine were mostly "I"-centric.

Foreignness isn't only a matter of speaking different languages. Although we were negotiating, my partner didn't even use the same rules as I would to try to modify my behavior. In fact, I learned that, in Japan, negotiation often has nothing to do with hammering out specific terms.

My employer at the time, the workstation company Sun Microsystems (now part of Oracle), sent me to Japan to negotiate the use of a Japanese company's fonts in our products. When my colleagues and I arrived at the Japanese firm's Tokyo headquarters, we went through the rituals of gift-giving and business card exchange. In Japan, this is a required form of showing respect and building goodwill—both elements of trust. (Before leaving the United States, I had learned how to properly receive a person's card, to take the time to examine it, and how deeply to bow. I was also advised by an expert to laugh at off-color jokes, even ones that might seem, by U.S.

standards, somewhat sexist.)

Our team had put forth a proposal for an agreement that covered every element, including pricing and warranties. We went back and forth on pricing, and our Japanese partners, not facile English-speakers, but attempting to negotiate without the benefit of translators, politely responded. I tried to convey the notion that the more we paid to distribute their fonts embedded in our software, the more legal warranties and indemnities we would require. Their team nodded in agreement, but what came from their mouths were platitudes:

"The warranty will be standard for your company."

"No need for to be concerned about quality of our products. Very high quality."

"Explain please indemnity."

We spent the entire day, with only a short break for lunch, working through the items on our agenda. As far as I could tell, we made no progress.

Then, around six, the entire Japanese contingency got up in unison and declared it was time for dinner. They took us to one of the most expensive restaurants in the city, and we sat cross-legged, toasting our partnership with sake glasses that kept getting refilled. We all told off-color jokes, never once talking business, and I started to relax.

When our meal was over four hours later, the men went off to a geisha bar, while my female colleague and I went back to the hotel. (We were invited along, but I had been taught that this was not a real offer and that I was expected to refuse, despite their repeated attempts to coerce me.)

The next morning my colleague called to advise me that the Japanese firm had accepted our proposal and would be getting us a new draft agreement to review later that afternoon. Despite my earlier thinking, the negotiations had not failed after all—they had somehow been converted (through sake and merriment) into success.

It turns out that in Japan, what happens in the corporate boardroom is often not as important as the bonding that takes place in a restaurant or bar.

In his book *The Japanese Negotiator: Subtlety and Strategy Beyond Western Logic*, Robert M. March emphasizes this point, which applies to all intercultural exchanges:

> To be a successful negotiator, one really needs first, to live in and understand the market that one is dealing with, not only from one's own viewpoint, but also from that of the other side. Second, it is important to understand the culture *and how local people usually negotiate with or influence one another.* Finally, success in negotiation does not evolve from having fixed ideas about the culture or its people, for ultimately every company you deal with, and every individual . . . from that company, is unique. You have to relate to the person, not to a stereotype that could lead you to treat all Japanese nationals as though they are the same.[7] (emphasis mine)

If you will be visiting your partner's territory, make an effort to learn permissible social behavior. It may seem to you that blowing your nose at the dinner table is perfectly acceptable, but to them it may not be. You may think that looking someone in eye is a sign of respect, but to them it may seem embarrassing or confrontational.

Similarly, when your negotiation partner visits you on

your soil, don't assume that they will understand or follow your culture's customs. Cut them some slack if they do something that would be considered inappropriate by American standards of negotiation or politeness.

As March tells us, understanding and accepting cultural differences also means avoiding stereotyping. I once watched a negotiation between lawyers for two strong, successful companies fall apart simply because one was from Denver and the other from Paris; each negotiation team looked at the other through biased eyes. The French lawyer was prejudiced against anyone who could speak only one language, served cafeteria food to guests for lunch, and wasn't willing to work past 5:00 p.m. The American lawyer assumed that the French were bureaucratic-minded technology hicks who provided poor customer service.

Everything unraveled when the Denver lawyer said, "You know, I've seen my share of license agreements, but this one is quite complicated and not very user friendly."

The Paris lawyer replied, "Well, perhaps if you had more experience with sophisticated customers from other countries, you wouldn't be so overwhelmed by our text, which no one else has complained about." Privately, she remarked to me in French that it wouldn't surprise her if the lawyer had never left Colorado or the United States. That was the end of the negotiation.

Culture can also shape a negotiator's style. For example, Eastern and Western negotiators typically deal with conflict in opposing ways. In the case of the Japanese negotiator, avoiding conflict and doing everything possible to "save face" is paramount. The Western negotiator, on the other hand, confronts conflict head-on using logic; other cultures may use emotion instead.

Some cultures are linear, some are circular. These are all issues to be aware of when negotiating with someone from a culture different from your own.

> **Try This:**
> Sit down with your partner and begin a conversation that has nothing to do with the negotiation. Instead, focus on trying to elicit as much as you can about your partner's background. Where were they raised? Where did they go to school? Do they speak other languages and have they traveled? How did they end up in this job?
>
> Share the same information about yourself. What you learn may not only facilitate negotiations with your partner, but also expose common ground upon which to build a relationship (and trust).
>
> During the negotiations, try to recall what you've learned before evaluating their positions or responses based on your linguistic or cultural or lens.

For an in-depth look at cross-cultural dynamics, I recommend reading Richard Lewis's book *When Cultures Collide: Leading Across Cultures*, now in its third edition. While not primarily focused on negotiation, he describes the behavioral, linguistic, and other anomalies that frequently occur among the hundreds of cultures he studied.

Finally, you may encounter a cultural difference in the form of a generation gap. William Strauss and Neil Howe, authors of *Generations: The History of America's Future, 1584 to 2069,* believe, among other things, that each generation has common characteristics that set it apart. For instance, in the context of workplace negotiations, it's common for managers from older generations to perceive younger workers as less motivated and engaged, or to criticize them for displaying a sense of entitlement. Again, be careful about stereotyping; my advice is to be aware of these perceptions, but accept each person as an individual. I remember a negotiation (performance management discussion) with a millennial employee who was very smart but who could not stay off his phone at work. The usual coaching methods were ineffective, so we sat down to talk more broadly about his goals. I learned that his phone was a lifeline; being networked in with friends and family was very important to him. I also discovered that he was bored with his job. We negotiated an arrangement: in exchange for limiting his phone time to approved breaks, I offered more responsibility and variety in the job, and a professional development class in accounting. The results were startling—he became a model employee—until he left for a better-paying job.

When you discover and address linguistic and cultural differences between you and your partner—not as a way to identify weakness or gain advantage, but as a way to bring the two parties together—you close one more negotiation gap.

CHAPTER NINE

Observe the Gender Gap

Is there a gender gap? Do men and women think and communicate differently? And, if so, do they tend to negotiate in different ways?

From a physiological perspective, the data support such differences. Brain scans show that the female brain processes language on both the right (intuitive/creative) and left (logical/analytic) hemispheres of the brain while the male brain processes language only on the analytic side. The female brain's centers for language and hearing have 11 percent more neurons; and the female hippocampus—the principal seat of emotion and memory, as well as the circuitry for observing emotion in others—is generally larger than in males. Neuropsychologist Louann Brizendine's book *The Female Brain* documents these phenomena.[8] Brizendine argues that brain structure and chemistry give women an edge over men in verbal skills, connection, the capacity to read faces and tones of voice for emotions, and the ability to defuse conflict. If women are generally better at listening and empathy, we have to question whether it's a fluke or biology that most human resource professionals are women.

In general, I've observed that men and women handle emotions differently as well. This supports Brizendine's thesis about the hormonal differences between the sexes. She contends that a typical male responds to emotions with a rational mind and with avoidance. A female on the other hand, tends to be in close touch with her feelings and is more willing to express her emotions. Hormones may also play a role in deciding when to negotiate, as we saw in chapter 6.

According to Brizendine, men and women also process anger differently: the amygdala—the center of anger and aggression—is usually larger in men than in women. But the center for control of aggression and anger—the prefrontal cortex—is typically larger in women. Finally, because of testosterone, men are generally more prone to aggression than women. We'll cover this topic more fully in chapter 23.

Though girls and boys start using language differently from a very young age—girls use more collaborative phrases; boys use commands, ignore others' suggestions, and override others' attempts to speak—biology alone doesn't end the debate when it comes to the gender gap.

Think back to the example of Peter and Maya negotiating where to eat dinner in chapter 3. Both their communication and their negotiation styles differed. Maya was more open-ended (conceptual), Peter more directed (task-oriented). They each also assessed the other person's response in distinct ways. Were these traits purely a function of their genders? Perhaps.

Could they also have been, at least partly, a result of upbringing, education, socioeconomic status, or other factors? Yes. Does the cause really matter in negotiation? No. What's important is that you understand your partner's method of communicating, recognize how that may differ from your own style, and use that knowledge to find common ground rather than let it create a chasm between you.

Let's move from the general to the specific now and address the issue of how men and women fare in negotiating salaries. I'm sure you've heard of the equity gap; it's the disparity in pay between men and women who perform the same tasks or hold equivalent jobs. One recent study claims that when women negotiate salary on behalf of themselves, they tend to ask for and receive lower rates than men.[9] This means that a woman who doesn't value her skills highly enough can start off with a gap of her own making. But if she does her homework, knows the salary range of the men doing the same job, and puts forth her qualifications, there is no reason why she can't successfully negotiate for what she deserves.

Negotiation outcomes may also vary based on external factors. In her book *Lean In: Women, Work, and the Will to Lead*, Sheryl Sandberg discusses the positive correlation for men between success and likability and the negative correlation for women. In the context of negotiations, this means that men are rewarded for negotiating hard for themselves in the workplace, while women are not. I have found that to be true in my own life.

Sandberg also writes, "The goal of successful negotiation is to achieve our objectives and *continue to have people like us*"[10] (emphasis mine). I disagree with the latter part of that statement. Most men don't think that way, so why should women? Negotiation is not a popularity contest. Yes, transformative negotiation may succeed or fail depending on the connections you develop with your partner, so it would be useful to maintain a cordial relationship after the deal is done. And I'm certainly not advocating that you negotiate with the intent of hurting others' feelings or making enemies. But women shouldn't have to apologize for negotiating a higher salary or worry about whether people will like them when they succeed.

There are many studies about gender stereotyping. One recent theory suggests that when negotiators view their female negotiation partners as less competent, they are more likely to mislead them. As we have seen, stereotyping of any kind is dangerous in negotiations, but this particular data, if validated, means that women are at a significant negotiating disadvantage. In a 2014 paper, professor Laura J. Kray and colleagues conclude that in buyer-seller settings, female negotiators are deceived more often than men, and conversely, male negotiators who hold these stereotypic views act less ethically in negotiations.[11]

It is well known that stereotype bias against women exists, conscious or unconscious. Who can forget the famous puzzle: A father and son are in a terrible car crash, killing the father and critically injuring the son. The son is rushed by ambulance to the nearest hospital. As he is being prepped for surgery, the surgeon walks into the room, takes one look at the patient, and exclaims "I can't operate on that boy. He's my son!" What is the surgeon's relationship to the boy?

But gender bias (or any other heuristic) should not be used to prevent us from exercising our inherent skills as transformative negotiators. Recall from chapter 4 that that any personal attribute can be—or can be transformed into—an asset. In negotiations, innate feminine attributes can contribute to a successful outcome, so can innate masculine attributes.

Here's a perfect illustration taken from a *New Yorker* magazine blog of what one person calls gender bias and I call overreaching.

Applying for a position at a college, W. (female negotiator) countered on an offer of employment with the following terms: higher salary, paid maternity leave for one semester, pre-tenure sabbatical, cap on the number of new classes she would teach each semester, and deferred start date. W. acknowledged her overreach but didn't see the harm in asking. Wrong. The college withdrew their offer, stating that they believed she would be better off teaching at a research university than at their smaller, student-centered college.

Was this the result of gender bias? I suppose one way to know would be if a man had made the same proposal (with paid paternity leave) and had been similarly rejected.

What W's counteroffer tells me, however, is that she didn't know her negotiating partner well enough. We've learned how important it is as a negotiator to view your terms from your partner's perspective. The college may have felt that W. was unwilling to do the work expected of new faculty or to put students first, properly justifying their rejection on something other than gender bias grounds.

I'm not sure this wasn't also about setting realistic goals (next chapter) and using leverage properly (chapter 20). Several of the proposed terms (pre-tenure sabbatical, cap on number of new classes) would best be negotiated *after* W. established a track record of positive evaluations; in other words, when she had more leverage. That is, unless she had matching offers, which is a different leverage analysis entirely.

If she needed more family time or better work-life balance (paid maternity leave), I expect W. to have reviewed the college's policies to see if they meshed with those needs. If they didn't, W. probably shouldn't have applied in the first place. If they did, she wouldn't have had to ask.

On the salary issue, I know it's hard to ask for more money, but my advice to anyone is to always include the *why*. Why should the college pay more? Did W. research salaries (men's and women's) of those in comparable positions and in her local market? Is she highly accomplished? Would she be more valuable to the organization than other candidates who might accept the offered salary? If so, how?

The point is, male or female, in any negotiation the key is to be fully prepared.

There are countless examples of prominent women enjoying success in negotiations. Here's one that highlights how a strong female leader/diplomat/negotiator might see and shape the world differently than her male counterpart.

In 2006, then–Secretary of State Condelezza Rice gave a talk at the Georgetown School of Foreign Service. In that speech, she discussed the principle of transformational diplomacy:

> I would define the objective of transformational diplomacy this way: to work with our many partners around the world, to build and sustain democratic, well-governed states that will respond to the needs of their people and conduct themselves responsibly in the international system. Let me be clear,

transformational diplomacy is rooted in partnership; not in paternalism. In doing things *with* people, not *for* them; we seek to use America's diplomatic power to help foreign citizens better their own lives and to build their own nations and to transform their own futures.[12] (emphasis mine)

Here we have the essentials of transformative negotiation: negotiating *with* partners rather than dictating *to* them. Looking for and working toward shared goals and common solutions. And perhaps most important, getting what you want by helping your negotiation partner get what he or she wants as well.

Women and men may have different brains, different ways of communicating and emoting, and, sometimes, different approaches to negotiation. But the gender gap isn't— or, at least, doesn't have be—a barrier to negotiation success. Observe the differences and adjust. A transformative negotiator, whether male or female, understands the value of connection and collaboration, and focuses on bridging gaps rather than widening them.

CHAPTER 10

Set Realistic Goals

Setting realistic, achievable goals is an essential part of any successful negotiation.

After a presentation I made at the *Working Woman* Entrepreneurial Excellence Awards, I met a client who needed help negotiating with a pharmaceutical company that was anxious to buy her domain name. Back then, in 2000, I had my own independent consulting practice and was happy to take her on as a client.

Before I began negotiating on her behalf, I researched the cost of domain names and came up with prices ranging from $100 to $100,000. (This was before the practice of "cybersquatting"— buying a well-known company's domain name and holding it for ransom—became illegal.) So we started with what she wanted to be paid, then factored in her current investment in the business, plus the future costs associated with changing her company name. The final number hovered around $20,000.

Many people had told her she could get over $50,000

through an Internet auction site, but I cautioned her against setting unrealistic expectations. With a live buyer on the line (whose corporate name matched her domain name exactly), my client agreed that I would first negotiate with this real brick-and-mortar company. However, she used the possibility of putting the domain name up for sale at auction as *leverage*, which I'll discuss in chapter 20.

The first offer from the pharmaceutical company was low—$17,500—but we used the leverage of the potential auction to raise the company's bid to well over twice that. Then it was up to my client. Did she want to take their offer or try to squeeze out more money in an auction, knowing that she would have to invest time and energy to auction the name? Moreover, there were no guarantees that she would find a buyer willing to pay more. In the end, she accepted their fair terms, they cut her a check, and she was happy.

In his book *The Art of Happiness*, the Dalai Lama explains the equation this way:

> You should never lose sight of the importance of having a realistic attitude—of being very sensitive and respectful to the concrete reality of your situation as you proceed on the path toward your ultimate goal. . . . Dealing with expectations is really a tricky issue. If you have excessive expectations without a proper foundation, then that usually leads to problems. On the other hand, without expectation and hope, without aspiration, there can be no progress.[13]

The difference between being realistic versus having hope is a matter of degree. For example, people apply for jobs every day that they know they aren't officially qualified for. I've done it myself—and succeeded. Unrealistic or aspirational? Each of us has to decide on a case-by-case basis.

Being realistic doesn't mean setting the bar lower or having a negative attitude about your chances of reaching your goals. Studies have shown that negotiators who express a positive mind-set and emotional state while negotiating are more efficient and successful than those who are either neutral or negative.[14] Your job as a transformative negotiator is to stay mindful and positive about outcomes while remaining grounded throughout the process.

I've seen people walk away from good deals only to face no deal. People price their houses too high. They reject a low but fair offer in the hopes of getting something better. They value their skills too highly. They understand their own value, but not the reality of the market.

In some cases, failure is inevitable. For example, you must have a starting salary no less than, say, $75,000 in order to survive in a particular location. Yet the job market in that location simply won't support such a salary.

A few years ago, part of my job at the University of New Mexico involved negotiating with prospective employees. We have a unique hiring model: we post our salaries in a range of low to high, with a midpoint. In the lawyer position we were currently interviewing for, our high was $110,000, with a midpoint of $75,000. We also have what we call an equity grid, which calibrates the salary range against the salaries of all our other employees with the same job title, adjusted for factors such as years of experience. In most cases, we cannot offer a person with certain qualifications and years of experience more money than a current employee with the same qualifications and experience earns. These were my parameters. Based on what the last lawyer in the position made, my equity calculations, and our budget, I was authorized to offer $90,000, with a little room to maneuver depending on special skills.

The candidate I was negotiating with was making $140,000 at a law firm but having to travel extensively, which he wanted to curtail.

I didn't understand why he applied for a job that required an immediate $30,000 cut in salary, but I had assumed that he had his reasons (location, family concerns, and so on). I had set the starting point for our negotiation not as his current salary, but somewhere within the salary range of our open position.

When we spoke on the phone, I mentioned that his legal experience put him slightly above the median and offered him $90,000. I highlighted all the nonmonetary benefits of the job—stability, no travel, and no billable hours—and he seemed to understand and value these trade-offs. He wanted me to include his business experience in the calculation, which I was not permitted to do and told him so.

He insisted on making $100,000 a year, not a penny less, and made a point of letting me know that it would be the lowest salary he'd ever accepted out of law school. I explained to him that I simply could not offer him that much, because it would have been unfair to others in the department with more years of experience. But he didn't listen. My assessment of his negotiating skills was not positive; I thanked him for his time and did not make a counteroffer. The negotiation ended, and I had to start the process all over again with another candidate—who, it turned out, was a much better negotiator.

When you understand and are honest about the reality of your situation, you help the negotiation proceed toward your—and your negotiation partner's—goals.

CHAPTER 11

Uncover Needs

Negotiation is communicating with another person with the intent of modifying his or her behavior to satisfy your *wants* or *needs*. A want is something that you would *like to* have, but it isn't critical. (Wants are frequently used as leverage in negotiations, as you'll see in chapter 20.) A need is something you *have to* have.

In any negotiation, both parties need to understand what each party must have. When these needs are clear, negotiations are most likely to proceed in the right direction (or to break off immediately when it becomes obvious that both sets of needs simply cannot be met through negotiation).

Please don't confuse need with *neediness*. You can express a need without being needy in negotiations. Several years ago, a client asked me to negotiate the purchase of a car; she had cash and wanted to drive off the lot with a specific Subaru that same day. As we drove to the dealership, I advised her not to reveal her neediness to the salesperson. She had to practice detachment, make the dealer compete for her money, and be willing to walk away if we didn't get a fair price. She followed my advice, and after investing time in the process, I negotiated with the salesman (alone) and got a good deal for her.

In most cases, your negotiation partner's wants are obvious: they want to sell their house on the best terms; they want to negotiate a decent salary; they want you to stop practicing your trombone with the windows open after 10 p.m.

But what about when you or your partner needs something that isn't clear or obvious?

I remember a negotiation to sell a piece of land I owned in Taos. I had decided that my perfect eight-acre plot was too isolated for retirement, so I put it on the market, hoping for a quick sale. After almost a year, I was ready to delist it when an offer came in, for $15,000 less than my asking price.

I bargained hard and we steadily narrowed the gap. When the buyer hit my idea of a fair price, we were ready to close.

But at the last minute, the buyer insisted on having the land resurveyed and wanted me to pay for it. I refused, because the property had been surveyed when I'd bought it two years earlier, and nothing had changed since then. I understood the buyer's need to have the land accurately staked, but I didn't want to cut any further into my tiny profit. And the truth was that I had gotten greedy.

Weeks went by with no movement on either side. My Realtor begged me to relent, but I instructed her not to give in.

Then I started to think about the bigger picture: About how nice it would be not to have the real estate in my portfolio. About how much stress was involved in trying to sell the property in a down market.

As I meditated on this conundrum, I finally realized that

one of my needs was peace of mind. When I saw that I might be giving that up for the sake of a few hundred dollars, I let go, agreed to the land survey, and signed the deal.

In this case, it took me a while to comprehend my own needs. Mindfulness practice and conscious breathing exercises can help in these situations, as we'll discover in chapter 15.

Here's an example of one negotiation partner not understanding the other's needs:

Back when I had my own law practice, I had a client who was a highly creative software engineer and inventor. He was the first to acknowledge that he was not a good businessman. He wanted me to negotiate the sale of either his company or the technology he had developed to a large media conglomerate. The deal was complicated by the fact that his previous lawyer had taken equity in his company and one of his business partners was being offered a high-level job with the media conglomerate.

The media conglomerate had already put a substantial financial offer on the table. But my client didn't want to take it.

He was ambitious, yes, but he wasn't looking for money alone. The things he cared most about were credit for his invention and continued validation of his skill as a programmer. However, the media conglomerate assumed the deal was all about money and that his reluctance to approve it stemmed from his desire for more. After all, his previous lawyer and business partner certainly wanted more. They couldn't fathom that for my client, money wasn't what mattered. As a result, the negotiations stalled.

I advised him to stop relying on go-betweens and, instead, to communicate directly with the media executives. I told him, "Let them know that you want to continue to be acknowledged for your invention and to receive credit for its future development."

After that discussion, the parties were ready to get back together and craft a deal that worked for everyone. This included appropriate acknowledgments for my client and putting him on retainer as a consultant for a year.

Sometimes your partners purposefully hides their real objective for the negotiations (as we saw in chapter 5), or you fail to understand their true need. Here's one more example of uncovering what your negotiation partner actually needs versus what you thought they needed:

Seventy-plus days into the 1979 Iranian hostage crisis, Hamilton Jordan, the White House chief of staff, met with an Argentine and a Frenchman, both representing Iranian interests. The discussion turned to the Shah of Iran, and what Jordan heard from these men was disconcerting. The Shah, he was told, must be returned to Iranian soil to stand trial; as long as the U.S. government harbored him, it was considered an enemy.

This directly conflicted with information Jordan had received from the State Department. On impulse, Jordan said as much. As Pierre Salinger observed in his book *America Held Hostage: The Secret Negotiations*, this was when the negotiations reached a turning point:

> He was a politician who dealt in give-and-take; every bone in his body was telling him that this was the moment to give. He turned abruptly to Bourguet. "We had thought all along that the real problem was the return of Iranian assets, and the taking up of relations between the countries on a new level, one of equality, where the Americans would promise not to interfere anymore in Iran. Okay. But we didn't understand that the problem of the Shah was that fundamental."[15]

Jordan was able to hear and understand his negotiation partner's true need. This breakthrough enabled the negotiations to move forward.

When either or both negotiation partners lose sight of the needs behind a negotiation, the entire process can be derailed. Bryan Burrough and John Helyar's book *Barbarians at the Gate: The Fall of RJR Nabisco* chronicles the financial saga of two unlikely partners, food and tobacco. As the drama unfolds, RJR Nabisco's CEO Ross Johnson decides to do a leveraged buyout (LBO) of the company. Once RJR Nabisco is put in play, however, everyone on Wall Street wants a piece of the action. Henry Kravis's LBO firm, Kohlberg Kravis Roberts & Co., pits itself against Johnson's management team for control of the company.

After a series of acrimonious and unproductive exchanges, the negotiations reach an impasse. Linda Robinson (principal at a PR firm specializing in corporate communications and wife of American Express CEO Jim Robinson) steps in. She decides the only way to break the logjam is to lock Johnson and Kravis in a room until they reach a compromise. The two men go into the room, but the negotiations fall apart. Here, in the authors' words, is why:

> It was all about egos, Linda Robinson knew. She considered herself finely attuned to the ways of her swaggering Wall Street clients. As so often happened, Peter Cohen and Tommy Strauss, and Henry Kravis and the rest had totally lost sight of their real objective, RJR Nabisco. Their disagreements had nothing at all to do with shareholder values or fiduciary duties. It was all a test of wills among an intensely competitive clique of macho, Park Avenue bullies in pinstripes.... Each was determined to be King of the Sandbox.[16]

Each man had a stake not only in winning, but also in being declared the one who pulled off the most lucrative LBO in history. This immovable attachment to ego turned the future acquisition of an American corporate giant into a cutthroat game of chicken.

Ultimately, Johnson lost and Kravis emerged victorious, but only at the expense of shareholders, employees, and a bloodied LBO industry. Everyone connected to both firms— except Kravis—lost big. This ego battle resulted in more than just financial losses and stock devaluation. It also depleted the humanity of the people involved and created much ill will and distrust.

We've covered the worlds of international diplomacy and high finance, what about one closer to home: the complex negotiations that take place in the realm of parenting.

I was starting my senior year of high school, not the least bit interested in attending college. My high school, Brearley, was one of the most prestigious all-girls schools in the country where every student was expected to move on to the Ivy Leagues, but my grades were mediocre. I vividly remember the heated discussions my parents and I had about college. My mother insisted that higher education was the path to success. She was in the process of getting a PhD in political science from Columbia University. My father also stressed the value of college, though he himself did not have a college degree. He was a self-made millionaire, who had already retired from the computer business.

While I could not articulate this at the time, I needed to be independent, and I viewed college as the path to staying dependent (not earning my own money) on my parents for another four years. I told them I did not want to attend, pointing to my father's success without pursuing a degree out of high school (he joined the Air Force) as proof that viable alternatives awaited me (even though I did not possess his skill in engineering and math). My parents needed me to gain higher levels of education to increase my chances of professional success in the future. But they expressed this need as a demand, rather than communicating their fear that my choice not to attend would severely limit my options down the road.

This example illustrates how underlying needs may escape direct expression and yet figure heavily into the situation at hand. We'll come back to this story later and see how a frame or leverage may be used to positively affect an outcome. Keeping focused on revealing the parties' ever-changing needs in negotiations can be as important as removing ambiguity and setting realistic goals.

CHAPTER 12

Construct and Reconstruct Frames

How a negotiation is framed sets the stage for how you act and how your negotiation partner responds. In a transformative negotiation, however, the frame is not just a frame; it encompasses the specific negotiation but also contains the vast universe, including connections, interdependence, and mindfulness as essential building materials.

In a legal brief, framing involves phrasing the central question to ensure (or at least encourage) the desired answer. For example, if you want the court to rule that prohibiting same-sex marriage is a violation of the equal protection clause of the U.S. Constitution, you might phrase your question as follows:

Does the Equal Protection clause of the Constitution, which prohibits states from denying persons the equal protection of the laws, render unconstitutional a state's attempt to define marriage as between one man and one woman?

If, on the other hand, you want the court to say "no" on that issue, your frame might look like this:

Do states have a legitimate interest in defining and regulating marriage, as they have for well over a century?

But a court case is not a negotiation, even when the parties are trying to persuade a judge or a jury. In a trial, the goal is not always a negotiated settlement, but rather a ruling in favor of one side, either the plaintiff or the defendant.

In a transformative negotiation, the frame needs to support not one particular need, but a successful outcome in which both parties' needs can be satisfied. This frame needs to be wide rather than narrow, and also flexible. If the frame is too narrow, you limit both parties' potential responses. Narrowness limits possibility; expansiveness opens it up.

Think back to the example of negotiating with your teenager to clean his room in chapter 1. If you frame it as a demand, you lose flexibility and the ability to find solutions. When you frame it broadly—gaining his trust instead of violating his privacy—you open up possibilities to find leverage and come to agreement.

Reframing can be quite useful in creating opportunities for leverage. As Herb Cohen observes in his book *You Can Negotiate Anything*:

> [D]on't define yourself too narrowly. Don't regard yourself as someone who wants to buy a refrigerator. Regard yourself as someone who wants to sell money. *Money* is the product that's up for sale. The more people there are who want your money, the more your money will buy. How do you get people to bid for that money? You generate competition for it.[17]

In the old days, car dealers set the frame of negotiations by putting a sticker on the car with the manufacturer's suggested retail price. However, this sticker price was marked up to provide the dealer with a profit. Now people know to research the dealer's *cost* on the Internet and start negotiations there, making the dealer negotiate upward, rather than negotiating down from the MSRP.

Fred Smith, chairman of Federal Express, has been hailed as one of the most innovative entrepreneurs of the last century. Smith knew how to frame. Initially, FedEx thought it was in the business of moving packages all over the world, but Smith saw his company's true purpose as bringing customers peace of mind. He broke the traditional frame in the shipping industry and replaced it with a much larger one, allowing the company to focus on a more substantive goal. And he built an empire assuring businesspeople they no longer had to worry "when it absolutely has to be there overnight."

It's even possible to reframe what people usually see as a drawback into a benefit, and vice versa. Here's one example.

In 1988, Sun Microsystems was looking to hire an experienced software lawyer. I applied for the job, even though I was only three years out of law school and hadn't done much licensing. I had, however, done my homework. I knew that Sun prided itself on being technologically open and culturally diverse, and that I was competing against senior candidates from more traditional computer companies.

In my job interview, I reframed the job requirements not around experience with software, but around compatibility with Sun's internal culture. In essence, I told the interviewer, "You don't want someone from IBM who's spent years picking up bad habits. Philosophically, I'm more aligned with open systems than with an old-school proprietary approach. Plus, I'm a hard worker from a good law firm. I've just come off six months of doing nothing but software licenses. And I'm a self-starter. Point me at the mess and I'll figure it out."

When my interviewer said, "I need a senior lawyer; you just don't fit the profile," I responded, "Eventually, I'll be senior. And in the meantime, you can mold me into someone who precisely fits your needs."

In this negotiation, I reframed my lack of experience *as an asset.* I also pointed out the drawbacks of my competition and highlighted my quick learning curve and malleability. My replacement frame was, *You won't have to break me of twenty years' worth of bad licensing habits, and you can count on my getting up to speed quickly.*

The frame held; I got the job.

Try This:
   Before you begin your next negotiation, think carefully about how you have framed yourself, your negotiation partner, and the negotiation itself.
   Are you framing the negotiation broadly or narrowly?
   How might you reframe any or all of these three to your advantage?

Mediators spend a lot of time reframing. If one party uses a phrase that frames, or presents, themselves as a victim and the other as a perpetrator ("when you screwed me over," etc.), the mediator tries to reframe the discussion in neutral, less emotionally laden terms (for example, by using factual "I" statements). If they don't, the victim may continue to feel victimized by the process no matter what the outcome, because he or she has already subconsciously given up his or her power to the other party. Through reframing, the mediator attempts to level the playing field. From this more neutral place, a new set of options often appear.

In the process of creating a new vision, reframing necessarily destroys an old one. This happened when I reframed "experienced software lawyer" as "stick-in-the-mud from IBM" during my job negotiation. And it happened when Fred Smith reframed the U.S. postal service as a source of anxiety and uncertainty for his customers.

Be willing to dismantle an existing frame if it is blocking your path forward.

CHAPTER 13

Validate Opposing Views

In many negotiations, both parties believe they are right, or at least reasonable. And often this is true.

Problems arise in negotiations not when the two parties believe they are right, but when either or both believe the other is wrong.

Physician, inventor, and author Edward de Bono proposed a thinking paradigm based on the idea of rock (or hard) logic versus water (or soft) logic. Rock logic is fixed and encourages rigor. Water logic, or perceptive and intuitive thinking, is soft and encourages change. He explains the difference between the two in his book *I Am Right—You Are Wrong*:

> In a conflict situation both sides are arguing that they are right. This they can show logically. Traditional thinking would seek to discover which party was really "right." Water logic would acknowledge that *both parties were right* but that each conclusion was based on a particular aspect of the situation,

particular circumstances, and a particular point of view.[18] (emphasis mine)

If both parties can simultaneously be right based on their unique circumstances and points of view, then what's the value of always trying to be right? What if, instead of relying on an exclusionary framework—on/off, right/wrong, true/false—we accepted the validity of both views? It is and is not. Not right versus wrong, but right in one way and right in another way.

Non-oppositional practice is hard. From birth on, we are trained to compartmentalize and categorize. It helps us cope; it helps the brain quickly react to the bad and savor the good. Yet it also creates a duality that doesn't necessarily exist. What does it really mean to say "right" versus "wrong"? In negotiations, it fixes positions and people on either end of an illusory scale and tends to encourage attacking the wrong/other. But if, as the Buddha taught, everything is mutable and impermanent, and we can see how we are all interconnected and interdependent, we can replace that rigidity with fluidity on the scale and flexibility of mind, body, and spirit.

Suddenly, a new, more expansive picture emerges.

Think back to the story in chapter 8 of the lawyers from Paris and Denver negotiating about licensing terms. The negotiation was hijacked by their judgment about each other's level of cultural sophistication. Both parties' positions and perspectives were "right," given their histories, upbringings, socialization, and work experiences. But can you see how it didn't matter which of them was "right" under those circumstances? The end result was a lack of trust and negotiations that ultimately devolved into litigation.

If we detach from our need for our negotiation partner

to be wrong, we can often accomplish much more. Declaring our partner wrong may appease our ego, but it does nothing to move the process forward. Remember, negotiation is about getting to a mutually satisfactory agreement, not about proving the other wrong.

In the case of the French client, had the Parisian not been so focused on proving that her partner was wrong about the license agreement she drafted, she might have responded more subtly, perhaps asking her to indicate which specific clauses were confusing. Or, better yet, she might have said, "You're right. Documents often lose clarity in translation from French to English." This would have gently blocked the criticism without hindering the flow of negotiation.

When we fail to view the situation in a wider context, we not only limit our ability as transformative negotiators to find common ground or come to agreement, but we also experience more difficulty developing compassion for our negotiation partner.

His Holiness the Dalai Lama addresses this principle of distorted thinking in his book *The Art of Happiness in a Troubled World*. He wrote, "The tendency to see things in absolute terms, as black and white . . . often lead[s] to inflexibility in one's point of view and the failure to see possible middle ground. There can also be a lack of willingness to look for common interests in a situation where we are trying to resolve conflicts through dialogue."[19]

In times of crisis, it is particularly tough to maintain an open heart and broad perspective, to resist the temptation of binary logic and oversimplification. The Dalai Lama goes on to briefly discuss an encounter he had with someone about the events of September 11, 2001. The U.S. government viewed the attack on American soil, the first since Pearl Harbor in 1941, as a clash of civilizations, the Western Christian (us) against the Muslim (them). These highly charged phrases, coupled with the "us versus them" frame, resulted in a polarization that made it challenging for people in the United States to even begin contemplating the root causes of the attack. What's more, this vision served to demonize an entire population. The Dalai Lama didn't agree with this distorted view of reality. Bin Laden was one man, yes a Muslim and an Arab, but he could not stand for the entire Islamic civilization any more than Charles Manson could represent the entire American generation of the 1960s.

This black-and-white thinking is prevalent in our society. And yet, can you see how counterproductive it is in negotiations? How can you solve the clash of civilizations or negotiate successfully with evil Muslim extremists? You cannot. But you might be able to make progress by dropping the rhetoric and looking at the entirety of the circumstances that culminated in the suicide attack on the Twin Towers: a group of individuals driven by hatred and resentment of a people it viewed as invaders. You do not have to agree with this view, but it helps to at least make an effort to understand it.

When one or both parties are solely focused on being right, the energy of intransigence permeates the entire negotiation. The transformative negotiator, however, understands how to re-vision the situation by validating all views, disconnecting from the extremes, and moving the parties closer to the middle.

CHAPTER 14

Check Your Perspective

In any negotiation, your perspective, like the frame, can be broad or narrow. It can home in solely on the parties and their immediate goals, or it can expand to include others who might be affected by the deal. It might also include the future of the negotiating relationship. Transformative negotiations require a more holistic perspective in the sense that they do not merely focus on scoring a win or getting to "yes." And as we saw in the last chapter, narrow perspectives can lead to closed minds.

Perspective can center a solution only on the present moment, or it can take into account the likelihood of changing circumstances.

Sometimes staying focused on the present moment is wise. I'm thinking of the Palestinian-Israeli peace process, which we'll look at in chapter 27. One of the reasons the process has repeatedly failed is that both parties insist on centering the negotiations on issues that, according to some, were resolved in 1967. Another cause of the breakdown is a focus on future events: Palestinians' right of return and the building of new Israeli settlements. A better early step would be to look at how the players can assist each other in supporting peace and prosperity *right now* in one contiguous land mass. This provides an opportunity for creating cooperation, trust, and success.

In other situations, a broader, longer-term perspective is best. Stepping back and viewing the situation in a wider context can help the parties more easily find an appropriate solution—or, at the very least, common ground. Often when people become fixated on minutia, it becomes impossible for other positive factors to exert an influence. Eventually, the focus on details can scuttle the entire negotiation, because people stop looking for common ground.

Here's an example of how a broadened perspective saved a negotiation:

I was negotiating with an engineering team at my company that was proposing to release free source code for a new software application on the Internet. Previously, the corporate office had rejected the proposal because it created too much risk with no immediate benefits (that is, profit). My job was to negotiate a solution that gave outside developers access to this source code, while protecting our intellectual property rights to the greatest degree possible.

My negotiation partner was the engineering manager. I'll call him Joe. We met in a hot, windowless conference room. Joe refused to allow any of the protections the corporate office needed. Every time I suggested adding a simple protective step, he'd nix it instantly. He told me that he had an engineering plan, blessed by his boss, that did not mention any licensing terms. To Joe, this document was a sacred text. To me, it was an albatross around my neck.

Me: "What if developers register via a website? They print out a one-page license, sign it, scan it, and send it back. We give them a password to download the source code. We're protected, and they get access."

Joe: "Won't fly. They need instantaneous access. No barriers to entry."

Me: "It'll take three minutes to print out a form, sign it, and send it back."

Joe: "Unacceptable."

Me: "Come on, Joe; be fair. This code won't get out at all if we can't find a compromise that satisfies corporate. They won't sign off without a license. Try to understand their point of view."

Joe (shouting): "You're wasting time. It's almost lunch and I'm having food brought in. Come back after we deal with the FAQ sheet and tech support issues."

I left the building and walked down the street. How would I keep the suits happy and bring Joe on board at the same time? I reviewed my proposals, all reasonable and feasible; I thought of Joe and his irrational refusal.

My mind went blank. All I could see was the used bookstore in front of me. I stood there for some time and simply breathed.

Suddenly, I knew how to protect the code without antagonizing Joe.

I had felt constrained in that windowless conference room, negotiating against a self-absorbed partner. By moving outdoors, slowing down, and *not* focusing on the problem, one part of my brain shut down and another part became activated.

I realized that I didn't need to negotiate with Joe at all, even though he'd been assigned as my negotiation partner. All I had to do was convince Joe's boss, a vice president, to embed a minimal set of license terms in the product itself. Then I wouldn't need

Joe's approval for anything, which would suit him just fine. Developers would get access to the code, and Joe would meet his goal of shipping the product on time, which I later learned entitled him to a sizable bonus.

That's exactly what happened. But this solution could not have been negotiated in that conference room with Joe. Instead, I had to adjust my trajectory and broaden my perspective—first by leaving the building, and then by removing Joe from the equation.

Try This:

In the purpose statement for your next (or most recent) negotiation, answer this question from your partner's perspective: why is Michele negotiating with me? That is, what does she want/need from me, why is she negotiating (her motive), and what is her walk-away point? This may help you clarify your own perspective.

When we're aware of our perspective and its limiting effects, we can change it. Even a subtle shift can move blocked energy, help us see things differently, and move the negotiation forward.

CHAPTER 15

Adjust Your Posture

One of the first things we learn in any physical activity—whether archery, ballet, or skiing—is proper posture. The same is true in a negotiation.

Your body language and physical stance can be as integral to the success of your negotiations as your persuasive ability. In fact, as negotiations drag on, the importance of these physical elements may increase exponentially. The more disconnected we get from our bodies, the more easily we can lose focus in negotiations.

How many times have you observed that crossed arms indicate a closed mind? What about the person who leans forward and pounds on the table to make a point, mistakenly equating noise and activity with authority?

Try This:

The next time you find yourself in the middle of an argument or disagreement, pause for a physical inventory. If you're standing, are your legs locked and rigid? How are your arms positioned? What are your hands doing? Is your jaw relaxed or tense? If you're seated, are you comfortable and balanced, or slumped or hunched over, or leaning back in shock? Are you looking at your negotiation partner or avoiding his or her gaze?

If your body isn't comfortable and alert, then, as soon as is practical, do whatever it takes to adjust—take a break, stretch, eat, adjust your clothing, or even adjourn the negotiating session.

Every few minutes, do a similar quick assessment of your negotiation partner's physical presence to assess receptivity to your message and pick up clues from body language.

Think of posture as a kind of meditation. Body awareness grounds you in the present moment.

Throughout any negotiation, try to maintain an open, flexible posture, with your muscles and brain alert but relaxed, your breathing calm and rhythmic. Your eyes and ears will now be ready to see and listen deeply, in a way that leads to understanding.

If you find yourself drifting, thinking of another matter, or wondering when you'll be able to take a break, you are not fully present in the negotiations. Bring yourself back to your body. Scan it, notice what you need to do, and make the necessary adjustments.

As you regularly center and re-center yourself, you will be

better able to maintain balance and flexibility, no matter what your negotiation partner does.

Negotiating when you're sick, tired, or hungry can be counterproductive. If your posture is suffering because of illness, hunger, or weariness, either adjourn or take a break as soon as possible and address the issue (have a snack, walk around the block, drink some coffee, or otherwise take care of yourself).

Here's an example of being completely off balance in a negotiation:

It was my first major deal at Sun. After months of negotiating by phone and fax, a British team flew to Silicon Valley on March 31 to negotiate the final points and to sign the contract no later than midnight, the end of their fiscal (tax) year. It was well after 6:00 p.m.; we were stuck on whether to use the European or American accounting standards for revenues. That's the conversation that was taking place in the room, but here's what was happening to me:

My head hurt. I had been trapped in an airless room for over nine hours without a significant break. The Brits contributed their cigarette smoke every time they came back from one of theirs.

I was hungry. Dinner wasn't brought in until after 7:30 p.m., and by then I had consumed way too much bitter coffee.

My feet were numb from wearing panty hose and pumps. I slipped my shoes off and tried to get the blood circulating, but I was unable to put my shoes back on. My feet had swollen up, and my toes were little red balloons.

Based on this physical inventory, I knew that (1) my brain was not getting enough oxygen, which made me lose focus; (2) my blood sugar had plunged, so I lost even more focus; and (3) my clothing was restricting my movements.

The result: hours after midnight, we signed a bad deal that ended up being terminated within the year.

When you stay awake to your posture and make a concerted effort to maintain it—as well as your overall physical, mental, and emotional health—during negotiations, your chances of coming to well-developed agreement increase.

Similarly, when you pay attention to your negotiation partner's posture, you will have some useful clues about the person's own thoughts, feelings, and physical state.

CHAPTER 16

Find Your Anchors

Negotiations are messy. It helps to have anchors—ways of grounding yourself. Two of the best are breathing and pausing.

Breathing

Most of us pay little attention to our breath, except when we lose it. We usually breathe shallowly, just enough to fill our lungs.

Breathing fully from our bellies helps us to maintain equilibrium. Breathing from the abdomen reconnects our head to our lower body, creating a thread between the logical mind and intuition. (According to Chinese medicine, our intuition resides an inch or so below our navel.) Abdominal breathing also helps prevent the mind from racing away with distracting thoughts.

> **Try This:**
> Take ten deep, slow breaths. Don't rush. As you breathe, become awake to each sensation, drawing air in through the nose, past the chest and lungs, and into the abdomen. Feel the expansion—put your hand there—hold the breath for a bit, and move energy out as you exhale.
>
> To get maximum benefit, engage your whole rib cage. Keep your spine relaxed but straight, adding a slight forward tilt to your pelvis.
>
> Medical studies have shown that deep breathing lowers blood pressure and oxygenates the cells. This in turn helps the brain function better.

Breathing is so important that Japanese writer Michihiro Matsumoto devotes an entire section to it in his book *The Unspoken Way*. The term *hara* to a Japanese negotiator means "big-heartedness, including caring, understanding, and tolerance for different views, gained through experience."[20] People of *hara* listen more than they speak, accept things as they are, and don't get personally or emotionally involved. And they breathe.

Matsumoto cites nine procedures for proper breathing in a negotiation:

1. Breathing must be deep. There are four types of breathing: with the shoulders, the chest, the *hara* (abdomen), and the toes. Deep breathing here means with the *hara*.

2. Breathing must be quiet.

3. Breathing must be long. You must learn to take as long a breath as possible.

4. Breathing must be steadily rhythmical. It must follow the rhythmic and repetitive pattern of exhaling-stop-inhaling-stop and back to exhaling.

5. Holding your breath [briefly, in between inhalations and exhalations] is as important as breathing itself, since it signifies *ma,* a breathing pause.

6. Breathing must be done in the correct posture. You must keep your spine as straight as possible but not tense.

7. Breathing must be performed to create energy. The energy created by breathing is called *prana* in yoga and *chi* in Taoism. Breathing, according to Shinto, purifies stains of your mind or *hara.*

8. Breathing must be done unconsciously. You must learn to get control of the rhythm of breathing until breathing becomes part of you.

9. Breathing must be done to discover yourself in the midst of nature. You must be able to develop your cosmic consciousness or identify with the mother earth through nirvana-seeking breaths.[21]

Long, slow breathing clears your mind and helps keep you focused. It also helps you stay calm and see potential solutions.

You can use your breathing as an anchor to avoid being uprooted by your negotiation partner's tactical ploys. Instead of crying "foul" or pushing back, just experience the discomfort of the ploy and keep breathing deeply. If necessary, count your breaths.

Whenever you feel irritated during a negotiation, pause briefly and focus on breathing deeply.

Pauses

Pausing in discussion, and allowing a few moments of silence to ensue, is a way to slow down the pace of negotiations. This creates space for clarification, reflection, and understanding. It also breaks (or at least dampens) the action-reaction-counterreaction cycle that can undermine a negotiation. Although this reactive state sometimes manifests in a professional or business setting, it is more likely to arise in a personal negotiation where in the heat of the moment, you say something you later regret. Pausing and breath are especially important in these circumstances.

Many of us are uncomfortable with silence in conversation, but silence can be helpful by forcing us (and our negotiation partner) to reflect on what has been said.

Transformative negotiators are as comfortable with silence and pauses as they are with speech. Indeed, when you incorporate pauses into communications, you will begin to notice that what hasn't been said might be as important as what has been. You may also become more aware of what needs to be said that hasn't been.

If your negotiation partner pauses, your job is to try to understand why. Is it deliberate? Are they searching for the appropriate word? Trying to fabricate a lie? What are they physically doing during the pause? Do they seem contemplative or agitated? Are they reaching for a glass of water, their iPad, or their briefcase?

Sometimes people pause to compose themselves when they feel emotional. If you suspect that to be the case with your negotiation partner, pay close attention to the person's words, tone, and body language immediately after the pause.

At other times, a pause may be an indication that someone

is running out of persuasive steam. This might be an opportunity for you to step in, change the dynamics, and gain the upper hand.

According to Matsumoto, pauses are critical to a Japanese speaker, but are often overlooked by Western negotiators:

> It seems to me that Western conversationalists listen to the words between pauses, whereas Japanese *haragei* practitioners listen more attentively to the pauses between the words and gestures. One doesn't need the art of persuasion that underlies Western communication practices to be a successful communicator in Japanese society. In fact, *haragei* performers are verbally inadequate in front of others, and by no means logical, coherent or articulate because they give *ma* (pauses and silence) full play. It is not surprising to learn then that the top salesmen of stocks, bonds, or insurance often turn out not to be smooth or slick talkers.[22]

By respecting *ma*, a speaker opens a space to achieve mutual understanding, gives the listener the time needed to process information, and offers the other an opportunity to interpret it.

Try This:
The next time you have a conversation, try focusing on the pauses. What do they tell you about what the speaker is saying, feeling, or trying to communicate? Then look at your own emotional and physical responses to the silence. Does it make you uncomfortable? What are you feeling? How is your body responding? Do you feel a strong urge to say something? Can you simply stay silent for a time, despite your discomfort?

> Try deliberately pausing when you want to emphasize something you've just said or to encourage your negotiation partner to reflect on it. What effect does this have on them? Does it increase the power of your last statement?
>
> If not, try repeating it; then fall silent and pause again.

Pausing can be a negotiator's best ally. It allows you to take a breath, digest what has happened, and refocus your energies. Pausing may also force your negotiation partner to stop and re-evaluate what he or she (or you) just said. The space often makes new directions and breakthroughs possible.

Pausing can also encourage questions or clarifications. It can emphasize the point you have just made. And it can be used to encourage your negotiation partner to make the next move.

CHAPTER 17

Keep Deadlines at Bay

When you set a deadline, it can give you leverage to gain concessions from your negotiation partner. Of course, when *they* set a deadline, it gives them some power to gain concessions from you.

There is nothing unethical about setting a negotiation deadline, but don't let a deadline trap you into making a bad deal. No deal is always better than a bad deal. Be willing let the deadline pass, or offer to extend it. Often, it's an artificial construct.

In fact, when you're negotiating, it's best to suspend your usual notions about time. Negotiate as if you have all the time in the world. Surprising as it sounds, this is often the key to reaching agreement.

Also avoid setting self-imposed deadlines in negotiations. Failure to meet that deadline may cause your reputation to suffer, even if the negotiation ultimately succeeds. What's more, if your deadlines slip, your negotiation partner may learn not to trust you fully or take you seriously in the future.

Think back to the British team who insisted an agreement be signed by midnight. As our negotiating session neared that hour, I had to wake my boss several times to get his approval of highly unfavorable terms. We finally ended up closing the deal at 3:12 a.m. But I had allowed their time pressure to weaken me physically and mentally, which forced me to make ill-advised concessions on behalf of my client. Once midnight had come and gone, I should have suggested breaking for the night and coming back in the morning, clearheaded and refreshed.

We usually think of deadlines as things that we set for ourselves and our negotiation partners. But sometimes deadlines can be set by circumstances, or other people, or even human error.

An unexpected deadline in resolving the Vietnam conflict provides a useful case history.[23]

During secret meetings in October 1972, a few weeks before the U.S. presidential elections, National Security Advisor Henry Kissinger agreed in principle to a nine-point plan submitted by North Vietnam to cease all hostilities. It was the first time the North Vietnamese had proposed a two-track negotiation: first end the war, then sort out the respective governments and boundaries of North and South Vietnam. Up until that time, the North Vietnamese had insisted that a military cease-fire be conditional on ousting the existing South Vietnamese regime. This change was a major breakthrough.

On October 26, about ten days before the election, Kissinger declared, "Peace is at hand," knowing that ending the war would all but ensure the president's re-election. But Kissinger wasn't focused on the success of those private negotiations; he was rushing the process to achieve an unrelated goal: a second term for Nixon.

Nixon was appalled by Kissinger's announcement, because he knew this created an artificial deadline to end a war very quickly. He publicly denied the existence of such a deadline, claiming he wanted a solid agreement, even if it meant waiting until after the election. But the damage was done, and the North Vietnamese used it to their advantage.

The plan's drafting was hurried and sloppy; some of the terms were ambiguous. Worse, Kissinger approved it without checking with Saigon. Not surprisingly, the South Vietnamese refused to sign off and asked for more time. Several delays were granted, causing the North Vietnamese to doubt Kissinger's word. Deadlines came and went without a peace deal; Nixon won re-election, but by the time Saigon agreed to a modified plan, the North Vietnamese went back to their original position, calling for the removal of South Vietnam's "puppet" government. Kissinger had to start all over. The parties endured another round of massive bombings before the end of the war was negotiated in January 1973.[24]

Don't make a commitment you (or the people you represent) can't keep. And even if you think you can meet a deadline—and manage other people's expectations—avoid announcing it prematurely.

Most people react negatively to deadlines and ultimatums. These imply that you have taken control of the negotiations and left your negotiation partner with few options or choices. Such a situation can create resentment and distrust. Furthermore, if you and your negotiation partner do miss the target, your credibility as negotiators will be diminished, whether you both walk away or agree to extend the deadline. This, too, may affect the degree of trust between the parties and make it more difficult to accomplish your goals.

CHAPTER 18

Build Trust

Trust is the lifeblood of any negotiation.

One way to think of trust is as a wave that starts with you and builds outward. It can flow from inside out *or* from outside in. It also has the potential for cumulative and exponential effects. (This paradigm comes from Stephen Covey's book *The Speed of Trust: The One Thing That Changes Everything.*)

Most of us trust those who are most like us, and distrust those who are not. In chapters 8 and 9, we looked at how to overcome linguistic, cultural, and gender differences in order to trust those who are not like us.

Trust is an essential element of transformative negotiation.

Trust can be freely given until it is broken, or it can be withheld until it is earned. Each of us has our own internal habit on this continuum—and these habits can change with the situation. In each negotiation, it's important to be aware of your own trust rules and to figure out those of your negotiation partner. Don't forget to factor in cultural differences; in some

Asian cultures, for example, protocols are more important than actions, and saving face is more important than keeping your word.

Try This:

Think of a person with whom you have a high-trust relationship. What does that relationship look and feel like? You can probably count on your partner cutting you slack the first time you fail to deliver on a promise or have a miscommunication.

Now think of someone you have a low-trust relationship with. What does that relationship look and feel like? If you fail to deliver, will the other person likely be forgiving? When you explain something to this person, how seriously will he or she take you? How accurately will the person hear what you say?

You can make trust more tangible by visualizing an account with credits and debits: the greater the number of positive interactions (credits) between you and your negotiation partner, the greater the degree of trust. Negative interactions result in withdrawals (debits) from the account, which reduces trust.

How do we go about building trust with a negotiating partner? Covey explains that the first wave of trust involves creating and maintaining congruence in your words, deeds, and motives. This means being a person of integrity, keeping your promises, and not being dishonest or deceptive. It also requires that you be competent and capable. If you represent an organization, person, or group, it means staying in close touch with them and accurately reporting their needs, wants, goals, promises, interests, positions, and agreements. In short, a transformative negotiator needs to be truthful, have honest motives, and have the skill and competence to deliver results.

In *Winners Never Cheat,* Huntsman notes that negotiators do not lose trust by "driving hard bargains, negotiating intensely, or fiercely seeking every legitimate advantage. Tough negotiations, however, must be fair and honest."[25]

Here's a brief story to illustrate. Huntsman was negotiating a deal to sell 40 percent of a division of his company for $54 million. It was a verbal agreement. In the six months it took the lawyers to write it up, his company value rose significantly; the division was now worth $250 million. His negotiation partner offered to split the difference with him and pay $152 million instead of $54 million, but Huntsman signed the original deal. Although it wasn't fair to Huntsman, to him it was more important to remain a man of his word; money clearly wasn't his sole motivator.

In the previous chapter, we looked at how Henry Kissinger and the government of North Vietnam tried to negotiate an end to the Vietnam War. Although fighting ultimately continued after the U.S. withdrawal in 1973, the cease-fire that was negotiated at this time would not have been possible had Kissinger not taken pains to establish trust with the North Vietnamese back in 1969. As Marvin and Bernard Kalb explain, "Somehow, he felt, if he could establish a sense of *personal trust* between American and North Vietnamese negotiators, he could break the deadlock at the Paris talks and end the war"[26] (emphasis mine).

To establish trust with the "other side," Kissinger had Nixon send a letter directly to Ho Chi Minh proposing negotiations between the United States and North Vietnam. He had the letter delivered by an unusual carrier, a French banker and former official in Indochina who had been on excellent terms with Ho since 1945. A week later, Hanoi officials approved a face-to-face meeting between Kissinger and Xuan Thuy, North Vietnam's chief negotiator. Thus began a series of secret meetings between the United States and North Vietnam that lasted many years.

The North Vietnamese team may not have initially trusted the Americans, but Ho did trust that the messenger they used would not deliver a proposal that was contrary to his country's interests. Once the channel was established, the two principals could begin the long, slow process of creating a direct personal bond.

Lack of trust is the primary reason negotiations fall apart. Mistrust breeds suspicion, and suspicion closes us down. If we do not trust our negotiation partner, we have little hope of succeeding. The same is true when our partner doesn't trust us.

Act with integrity and keep your promises, know and honor your partner's trust quotient and meet his or her expectations, and you will lay a strong foundation for a successful and transformative negotiation.

CHAPTER 19

Trust Your Gut

Many people use the terms "instinct" and "intuition" interchangeably. Others think of instinct as something we're born with—a physical trait—and intuition as something more cerebral that develops with experience. The Latin root of intuition roughly translates as *to look inside*, or *to contemplate*. The Latin root of instinct is *to incite* but is defined as a natural impulse, or a reaction not based on thought. Both instinct and intuition share a certain trait: the absence of analytical, linear thought. Some people call it "trusting your gut."

The neocortex of the brain is responsible for rational, analytical thought and language. The limbic portion of the brain is responsible for feelings such as trust, but is not connected to the language center of the brain and this is why it's often so difficult for people to put their feelings into words. Thinking something is wrong is not the same as feeling it is. How often have you heard someone say, "I should have listened to my heart" or "Why didn't I go with my gut?" after making a poor decision.

Yet the limbic brain, while speechless, is by no means powerless. It drives most human behavior, often behavior that flies in the face of neocortical logic. Your negotiation partner may be saying and doing all the right things, yet instinctively you may feel the person is not being honest with you.

The transformative negotiator uses all areas of the brain, integrating the rational with the intuitive to negotiate from a balanced inner space.

Think back to Hamilton Jordan's negotiations to release the American hostages in Iran. Here's what ran through his mind when he admitted his ignorance about the true reason for Iran's request that the United States return the Shah:

> [A]nd in that moment it occurred to Jordan that he had just made the most undiplomatic admission in the presence of the representatives of Iran. But it occurred to him, as well, that conventional diplomacy had gotten them nowhere for seventy-seven days. He was not a professional diplomat but he was the man they had asked to deal with because they liked the way he operated. The way he operated was to *trust his instincts*, and he was going to trust them now.[27] (emphasis mine)

Notice that Jordan didn't see himself as a "professional diplomat," but as a man chosen for his skill. And his intuition in that moment told him not to argue, not to try to defend the U.S. information and/or position, or to insist that it was right. He understood that things were not as straightforward as he had previously thought, and he put his analytical mind on hold and let his instincts take over.

Back when I had my own law practice, I was contacted by a

businessman who was looking for a lawyer to help his company with a number of matters. I agreed to meet at his office, fully prepared to pitch my firm for the job. I did my homework on him and his company, learning as much as I could from publicly available information, and figured out what legal services he might require.

As soon as I sat down, he started questioning me intensely. We had already agreed, as was my practice, that the first half hour of consultation was free. He asked for a list of clients (good practice) and tried to get answers to specific legal questions, which I was unwilling (and unable) to do without a signed engagement letter. He wanted to know about my billing cycle, if I would negotiate a (lower) hourly rate, and how available I would be to him. He warned that he might need to call me after hours. These queries all seemed reasonable.

I replied clearly and cordially, offering local references and trying to put him at ease. The man was clearly smart and ambitious, and he had a huge book of business to offer—but something didn't feel right. I started getting an unpleasant feeling in the pit of my stomach, a nagging sensation that connected my belly to my head. It told me, "Walk away."

He finally paused long enough for *me* to ask a question.

"How many lawyers has your company worked with in the past?" I blurted out.

This was not a rational question. It wasn't even a very diplomatic one. It came from my limbic brain struggling to make sense of the feelings I was experiencing.

He hesitated for a moment, then launched into stories about all the lawyers who had let him down, who had been unresponsive, or who had gouged him. He'd had to fire four lawyers. I was to be lawyer number five.

"Frankly," I said, "I'm not sure I'm the right person for this job."

I know I left a lot of money on the table. But my gut—that is, my limbic brain—told me that this man would be very high maintenance and probably litigious. And I—that is, my neocortex—reasoned that the consequence of having a client with unreasonably high expectations would take its toll on me.

I later discovered that the man had repeatedly sued his prior law firms over billing and made reports to the local bar association of his lawyers' alleged unethical behavior.

When you're a transformative negotiator, heeding your intuition is sometimes as important as applying your best logic or reasoning. And sometimes it's even *more* important.

CHAPTER 20

Apply Leverage

Wherever there is value or importance to the other party, there is leverage for you. The word "leverage" sometimes has negative connotations; it's seen as a way to force others into acquiescing against their will. But transformative negotiators don't use blackmail, ultimatums, or lies to come to agreement. We know how to use positive leverage wisely and how to look for and find it in unexpected places.

Finding Leverage

Money is the undisputed king of all levers. But just as the King of Norway wields no power in Jordan, and vice versa, money has its limits. Indeed, many items in a negotiation may have significant emotional, spiritual, or strategic value to you and/or your negotiation partner.

Here are some examples of nonmonetary levers:

A job offer from another potential employer, used to gain a sought-after promotion or a better salary and/or benefits in your current position.

A salesperson's attention. The more time and energy a salesperson invests with you, the more likely you are to reach a fair bargain.

Your voice, raised in a crowded shop: "Is this the way you treat customers? I'd like to speak to the manager, please."

A boycott, as in throwing tea into the Boston Harbor to protest taxation without representation.

The collective voices and actions of many, used to persuade corporations or lawmakers to do (or not to do) something.

The power of publicity, both good and bad. When Häagen-Dazs (owned by Pillsbury) waged an ice-cream war against upstart Ben & Jerry's, Ben & Jerry's created a publicity campaign that asked, "What's the Doughboy afraid of?" Ben & Jerry's also printed an 800 number for the Doughboy Hotline on packages of its ice cream and took out related ads in print and on billboards. The media soon spread the story. Seeing that Ben & Jerry's would not be intimidated and, concerned with its own squeaky-clean image, Pillsbury backed off.

Your status as an underdog. See above.

Your negotiation partner's concern with its public image. See above.

Your negotiation partner's competition. You can talk about going to a specific competitor or, as in the domain name example in chapter 10, you can leverage your willingness to make a deal with the highest bidder.

The threat of legal action, provided it is not frivolous or unsubstantiated.

Concessions and compromises. Use your give-ups to add to your gains. If you've made one big concession, leverage it to get many smaller ones from your negotiation partner. Keep coming back with, "Well, I did accept a lower fee" (or a higher cost, or whatever).

A willingness to walk away—and the wisdom to know when to do it and when not to.

A deadline, provided it is used wisely, and not capriciously or ruthlessly.

The timing of an event. When New York City's garbage collectors go on strike, they typically do it in August. What could be better leverage than plastic bags piled high on every sidewalk, allowed to bake in the sweltering heat of the city? Within days, those enormous, smelly trash piles turn New Yorkers into angry, impatient allies of the garbage collectors, and disputes are settled quickly in the union's favor.

You can sometimes pull leverage out of thin air. But be mindful. Deception has no place in transformative negotiations; I'm not suggesting that you lie. In fact, don't. You will get caught, your reputation will suffer, and no one will trust you.

There are times when people will use deception and orchestrate a negotiation to give the impression that they have what their partner wants, as means to getting what they want. This tactic occurred multiple times in the movie *The Negotiator*, with Kevin Spacey and Samuel L. Jackson.

In the movie's final scene, Kevin Spacey's character, Chris Sabian, negotiates with a corrupt precinct captain and lets him believe that Sabian has collected evidence of the captain's wrongdoing on CD-ROMs. When they agree on Sabian's buy-in price to protect the captain and continue the cover-up, he hands over the discs, and the captain breaks them into pieces. But the discs are actually blank, and the entire negotiation is secretly broadcast on a hidden radio. In the end, Spacey's character gets what he negotiated for: a public admission of guilt from the captain.

For best results, use multiple forms of leverage at once—or, depending on the negotiation, in sequence.

Try This:

Before your next negotiation, sit down in a quiet space and meditate for an hour on the negotiation. Let's say you want a job with a technology company and you have found a posting for an open position at a fabulous company, but as a recent college graduate you don't have the experience they're after.

Forget about the stated qualifications. Meditate on the following: Who are you and why are you unique? What classes did you take? What connections do you have? What volunteer activities did you engage in over the last four years? Did you travel?

Write out your strengths and weaknesses and why you want the job, as we did in chapter 4. Be sure to write your purpose statement from your standpoint as well as from the standpoint of the company.

Find out everything you can about the company and try to match your skills, knowledge, and abilities to their needs. Be sure to think broadly at both ends—for example, they may need to hire more minorities or women, or your minor in sustainability studies may set you apart.)

Now think about leverage. Obvious: Do you know anyone in the industry (or the company) who could be a potential reference, mentor, or champion for you? Can any of your professors help? Are there any networks or associations you could join to show interest in the company

---

> or its business (and meet people)? Non-obvious leverage points: Does the company offer internships? What kind of competition are you facing and how can you differentiate yourself (for example, you're young, energetic, and malleable)? Are you willing to take the position at a lower starting salary and work your way up in some agreed-upon time frame?
>
> You get the picture.

When You Have No Leverage

What do you do when your negotiation partner hands you a contract and states that it's non-negotiable? My advice is to walk away.

Negotiation is about coming to consensus so that both parties get what they need or want. If your partner is unwilling to negotiate with you at the outset, he or she probably will not be remotely concerned about your needs in the future.

A few years ago, I was looking to publish my first novel and had heard about a company that might consider it. I sent in my manuscript, which was accepted, and the company sent me a completely one-sided contract. I sent back an email with my proposed revisions. The company's response was, "Sorry, we don't make changes to our contract."

I decided not to sign. Then I did a Google search on the company. The first five hits revealed dissatisfied writers complaining that the company didn't live up to its commitments.

If I hadn't walked away, I might still be fighting to break a bad contract.

Losing Leverage

Here are some ways you can lose leverage in a negotiation, if you are not mindful:

Negotiating money separately from the rest of the terms. You're at a distinct disadvantage when you negotiate any part of a deal in a vacuum. It's vital to maintain the integrity of the whole exchange. For example, how can you assess what you're willing to pay for an item unless you know what risks you're taking? Is it fully warranted for a lifetime, or for a year—or is it offered as is, without any warranty at all?

Giving away too much early in the negotiation. This can leave you with little or nothing to trade when the time comes to negotiate on the issues you care most about. Hold something in reserve.

Framing the negotiation too narrowly. In the Ben & Jerry's example above, the specific dispute was between two successful start-up companies, Ben & Jerry's and Häagen-Dazs. But then Häagen-Daz was bought by Pillsbury and the frame (and possible levers) expanded. It became a fight against Pillsbury: not one ice-cream company against another, but the Fortune 500 company against two hippies.[28]

Being unprepared for your negotiation partner's response to your use of leverage. Put yourself in their place and think through what they might do and how it might affect you. Then prepare and rehearse your response.

Not identifying all your potential levers. Think back to the story of the negotiations with my parents over college. I failed to recognize their underlying fear, but they knew me and properly interpreted my reluctance as cover for wanting more independence. And they came up with a brilliant plan.

If I applied and got into college, they would buy me a car. The type of car would depend on the quality of the school I attended. Now keep in mind that I lived in Manhattan and never saw the need for an automobile in the city. And also note that I still had the option of not applying, but now I would be depriving myself of my first set of wheels. This lever quickly propelled the negotiations forward. I began to think of leaving home and the freedom associated with having a car. And I started applying myself to schoolwork and writing college application essays. In 1977, I became the proud owner of a brand-new silver Chevy Camaro with a red racing stripe.

Not using multiple levers at once, when doing so might be both helpful and prudent.

Leverage is the secret to moving seemingly immovable objects. Use it wisely and thoroughly, and look for it everywhere you can.

CHAPTER 21

Address Power Imbalances

What happens in a negotiation when the parties start off with unequal bargaining power? What are the typical advantages and pitfalls of this situation? What can cause the power imbalance to shift, and what are the ramifications of such a shift?

The story of the Taos Pueblo's battle for the sacred Blue Lake watershed—a series of negotiations that lasted over six decades—offers some profound insight into these questions.

It started in 1906 when, with the stroke of a pen, Teddy Roosevelt stripped the Tewa Tribe of its aboriginal title, gave their sacred watershed surrounding Blue Lake to the federal government, and made it subject to United States Forest Service policies. Those policies centered on multiple uses, which included recreation, the exploitation of resources, and grazing. Only by maximizing each use, the Forest Service insisted, would the land create optimum value for all citizens of this country.

These policies ran directly contrary to the tribe's, which

were centered on the interrelationship of land and people, and the sacred trust created by this bond. Only by protecting and paying homage to the land, the Tewa believed, would the land in turn protect, sustain, and nourish the tribe.

The tribe spent the next sixty-five years trying to regain title to their land. Not just use permits; not just the return of parts of the watershed; not just monetary damages as reparations; but the unconditional return of full ownership and full control.

The negotiations resulted in many conflicts along the path: among tribal members, with and among the multitude of attorneys and other agents representing the tribe, with and among representatives of the Forest Service, and among all three branches of the U.S. government.

The cooperative agreement the tribe negotiated in 1927 with the Forest Service was far from genuinely cooperative. The Tewa Indians had the right to patrol the property and keep out non-Indian visitors, except those given permission by the Forest Service. But the Forest Service took care of everything else, ostensibly with an eye toward protecting the secrecy of the tribe's religious rituals. The Forest Service approached the negotiations leading to this agreement with arrogance, even with hubris. The tribe signed this unequal agreement, believing it was all they could hope for at the time.

Yet the Forest Service's arrogance only sharpened the tribe's long-term resolve. They knew that their rights under the 1927 use permit were too tenuous, subject to the whim of petty bureaucrats, and potentially revocable at any time. Anything less than title to the land would leave their sacred charge exposed.

Rather than walking away or giving up, some Tewas refused to concede their lack of bargaining power. The tribe began to think bigger about how to get what they needed over the long term.

As the years passed, they continued to negotiate with the Forest Service, but they also initiated a multipronged campaign to create favorable national legislation and to develop a base of support. The tribe used local and national print media and, later, television to bring attention to the government's treatment of Taos Pueblo land. They sent a booklet of information to one hundred editors of leading newspapers. This coincided with the introduction of the tribe's first bill in Congress in 1966.

Soon afterward, ABC-TV did a special on Blue Lake, further increasing the tribe's sphere of influence. In 1967, every visitor to the Taos Pueblo was asked to help by contacting their senators and urging them to pass the bill.

The tribe also used a variety of other levers. In negotiations on water and land projects with the town of Taos, various local associations, and other organizations, the tribe routinely withheld its permission until its negotiation partner agreed to support the Blue Lake legislation. This support led to endorsements from the Taos Town Council, the local soil conservation district, New Mexico's Commission on Indian Affairs, and the National Congress of American Indians.

Use of leverage gradually caused the power to shift in favor of the Tewa Tribe.

The tribe had seen how the Forest Service's narrow frame had limited their chances of getting what they wanted. So they also worked to widen that frame.

The Forest Service had viewed the negotiation in terms of the claims of self-interested Indians versus the rights of U.S. citizens to enjoy their public lands. But the tribe had always believed they were negotiating for religious freedom--that Blue Lake was its church, and failure to return it would cause the Indian way of life to die. Using this frame, in 1967, the Tewa Tribe gained the support of the National Council of Churches and the New Mexico Council of Churches.

Over the years, people in authority changed, but the Tewas continued to push for the return of Blue Lake.

When Richard Nixon became president, the tribe saw another opportunity to exert its nascent power. Nixon strongly favored Indian self-determination. For the first time, the Tewas rallied the executive-level power of the U.S. government to their Blue Lake cause. On December 2, 1970, the Senate voted 70–12 to return full control of Blue Lake and the surrounding areas to the Taos Pueblo. The bill was signed into law on December 15 of that year. It not only righted the government's original wrong committed in 1906, but also set meaningful precedent for other tribes seeking redress for previously taken lands, and acted as a model of persistence in the face of difficulty and staunch opposition.

Did the Tewa Tribe set an unrealistic goal of not stopping until they once again controlled title to the entire sacred watershed? No. Instead they applied a unique form of leverage— their elongated sense of time—and a persistence that has lasted generations. As a result, they prevailed.

Blue Lake is the story of a paternalistic government exercising its bargaining power over a weaker negotiation partner, and ultimately being out-negotiated. There are countless similar illustrations of this in history. The Americans seminal struggle to negotiate the nation's freedom from Great Britain is one. Another is the Tibetans' ongoing negotiations with the

Chinese over sovereignty, which may eventually tip in Tibet's favor.

Similar power imbalances within companies and other organizations have often spawned unexpected outcomes, in which the ostensibly weaker negotiation partners ultimately came out ahead or were able to negotiate more favorable terms than most people thought possible.

Be aware of power imbalances—and the possibilities for creating subtle (and not-so- subtle) power shifts—in negotiations. These power shifts, especially if they accumulate over time, can help you achieve your negotiating goals, even in the face of great opposition or terrible odds.

CHAPTER 22

Practice Humility

In 1989, before heading to Tokyo to negotiate with Japanese customers, I attended a three-day class called Doing Business with the Japanese. On the very first day, a woman walked into the conference room and set her briefcase down at the head of an oblong table. When the group had quieted down, she began with a description of her credentials. To us, it sounded more like an apology.

"I'm relatively new to this and haven't had much time to prepare. But I'll gladly share what little I know about negotiating with the Japanese." She paused, then went on in the same self-deprecating vein for several more minutes. Then she ended with a bow and asked this simple question:

"What did you think of my opening remarks?"

A financial analyst answered, "Well, you sound unsure of yourself. Just how long have you been working with the Japanese? Are you qualified to teach us this stuff?"

She smiled. "Thank you. You're quite right, Frank. I've

just demonstrated the primary method of negotiation used by a native Japanese speaker. He humbles himself. We Americans want to help and may even feel superior to him. And we're ready to exploit his weakness. But in reality, the speaker knows way more than you do. He just doesn't want you to know that he knows."

Deference and humility are prized traits in many Eastern cultures. The theory is that if you think you are stronger and in a better bargaining position than your negotiation partner, you will be required to help them—the weaker, less well-positioned party—by offering concessions. It's a strategy that also works in North America.

What do I mean by "humility"? The most common definition is *modesty*. But the Latin root of the word can be translated as *grounded*, or *from the earth*.

In the United States, being humble is often confused with being weak. But humility and assertiveness can and do coexist. In his book *Negotiating International Business*, Lothar Katz says, "While the Hong Kong Chinese view politeness and humility as essential ingredients for a successful relationship, these factors do not affect their determination to reach business goals."[29]

In Stephen Covey's view, "A humble person is more concerned about *what* is right than about *being* right, about *acting* on good ideas than *having* the ideas, about *embracing* new truth than *defending* outdated positions, about *building the team* than *exalting the self*, about *recognizing contribution* than *being recognized* for making it."[30]

In other words, humble people put others first and are willing to expose their vulnerabilities. Adam Grant, in his book *Give and Take*, recognizes humility as a characteristic of a giver (as opposed to a taker or matcher). In his terminology, a giver engages in "powerless communication," listening, asking questions, admitting weakness, and seeking advice. He cites the disarming trial lawyer with a stutter as an example. In Jim Camp's world of "no," the successful negotiator has to "not be okay," less than perfect, in order to make his or her negotiation partner feel more at ease. His example is the disheveled detective from the *Columbo* television show. In both cases, people will empathize with a negotiator who is imperfect and may instinctively trust that person a bit more.

Humble people have been successful in some of the most influential negotiations in history. Think of Nelson Mandela who, in a complex, multiparty setting, after serving twenty-seven years in prison and against a backdrop of political and ethnic violence, negotiated an end to apartheid in South Africa.

Or consider Benjamin Franklin, the consummate negotiator, who knew the value of using silence and humility in presenting his position. His ownership of a printing press allowed him to persuade others indirectly, through essays often written under pseudonyms. He also credited others with significant ideas. (But Franklin was not without his detractors. Many believe that he was anything but humble, and he often used others' words without permission.)

Regardless of how you judge his behavior, Franklin was responsible for several important and successful negotiations, including getting a treaty signed with the French to aid America against the British during the Revolutionary War, negotiating peace with Britain at the war's end, and helping to create the U.S. Constitution. One of his many biographers, Walter Isaacson, summed up his contributions this way:

He believed in having the humility to be open to different opinions. For him that was not merely a practical virtue, but a moral one as well. It was based on the tenet, so fundamental to most moral systems, that every individual deserves respect. During the Constitutional Convention, for example, he was willing to compromise some of his beliefs to play a critical role in the conciliation that produced a near-perfect document. It could not have been accomplished if the hall had contained only crusaders who stood on unwavering principle.[31]

It takes great strength to be humble in negotiations, to give more than you take and to put others' needs before your own. But this is the level of selflessness a transformative negotiator must aspire to. In Buddhism, a Bodhisattva is a person following Buddha's Noble Eightfold Path, who helps relieve the suffering of every sentient being in the world before trying to achieve his or her own awakening. This capacity for humility goes hand in hand with empathy and compassion, which we'll cover in the next chapter.

CHAPTER 23

Manage Anger

A nger is the most common emotion in negotiations.
In and of itself, anger is not a problem. It's what you do
with it that matters. You can use anger to disrupt a negotiation
or as a catalyst for positive action against injustice.

Because transformative negotiators are grounded, they
can't be uprooted by anger—either their own or others'—just as
they don't react to triggers, judgments, or emotionally charged
words.

Anger is a real feeling, and I don't mean to imply that you
shouldn't experience it fully, if that's what comes up for you in
the moment. But it may not be appropriate or helpful to express
it to your negotiation partner. Acting out of anger is rarely
effective in getting another person to modify his or her behavior
to satisfy your wants or needs. Indeed, when you express anger
in a negotiation, you can lose your leverage. You can also lose
the trust of your negotiation partner.

Expressing anger can derail a negotiation, especially with

negotiation partners in Asia, who believe that hiding (or not showing) emotions is a matter of good negotiating etiquette. Harmony among partners must be maintained at all costs, and your ability to stay calm is linked to your reputation. Causing embarrassment to your partner—for example, by getting angry in front of others—can lead to a loss of face that spells disaster for the negotiations.

Depending on your gender, as we saw in chapter 9, expressing anger may come naturally. No matter what your gender or ethnicity, however, when strong emotions erupt, communications can break down. As a result, we can get drawn into a vortex if we don't know how to use anchors to stay rooted (as we learned in chapter 16), if we don't have good boundaries, or if we don't adapt to unexpected developments.

Boundaries are crucial. If you keep the negotiations focused on the parties' interests, angry energy won't penetrate, because it's not personal to you. In effect, you're holding up a mirror in the negotiation and saying, "This is about you, not me. If you're feeling anger, work it out on your own time, not here in the negotiation."

If you're confronted with your negotiation partner's anger, neither get caught up in it nor close down in response. Instead, stay open and assume the role of observer. Let your partner's energy rise and fall with your conscious breath, as we practiced in chapter 15. Adjust your posture; take a time-out, if necessary. Above all, be compassionate. Even when your negotiation partner is being disrespectful, your empathy can help to deflect that energy.

Here is a story illustrating how anger disrupted, but did not destroy, a negotiation I was involved in. A technology company wanted to license a pre-release version of Sun Microsystems' speech recognition software. We met at their offices in Santa Cruz to negotiate the deal. The session started amicably. We discussed deal points, what we had to offer, and how much they were willing to pay. I was honest about our needs, and so was their lawyer. I'll call him Charlie. I thought, "This will be easy."

Then we hit an obstacle: the patent indemnity. An indemnity is a form of insurance against loss that forces the seller to protect the buyer from lawsuits. Charlie wanted it, and I didn't want to give it to him. We went back and forth about industry practice and who should bear the risk. When I offered a limited indemnity, Charlie suddenly lost his temper. He raised his voice and pounded on the table. "That's not the way this is gonna play out. You think just because you're a big company you can push us around. Well, I'm not letting it happen."

At first Charlie's outburst didn't bother anyone. It seemed like a momentary lapse. But he didn't stop. He kept shouting at me and taking cheap shots at my company—and he never explained why the full indemnity was so important to him. He went on at length, getting steadily louder. Meanwhile, his clients scribbled notes to each other.

In that moment, I had great empathy and compassion for Charlie. Compassion is one aspect of Right Thought, the second step of the Noble Eightfold Path in Buddhism. Here's a beautiful passage from Goldstein's book *Mindfulness* on the subject:

> Compassion is the antidote to this great destructive power [cruelty]. Compassion is the strong wish of the mind and heart to alleviate all suffering. It opens our hearts to the suffering that is there, and it overcomes our indifference. It is the strong and deep feeling that

is moved to act. As Thich Nhat Hanh so aptly put it, "Compassion is a verb." And it was this very feeling that motivated the Bodhisattva on his long journey to Buddhahood.[32]

I knew that Charlie's anger didn't have anything to do with me personally, and I didn't absorb any of his negative energy. Instead, I took a deep breath, stayed open, and said, evenly, "Charlie, I can't hear what you're saying when you're shouting."

Charlie stopped shouting. His client asked for a few minutes alone with him—an ironic reversal of the lawyer doing damage control for the client. I left the room.

During the break, I learned why Charlie had to insist on a patent indemnity. The vice president—his client—pulled me aside and told me in confidence that the company had been sued for patent infringement. The litigation was sucking huge chunks of cash from their bottom line. I thanked him for being honest about the situation.

Instead of simply and clearly articulating his fear of being dragged into another lawsuit, Charlie had lashed out at me. His anger nearly scuttled the negotiation. Maybe he needed permission to disclose his concerns—in which case he should have sought it. Then I could have taken the proposal back to my leadership to see if they'd be willing to make an exception in this case. Or we could have spent our time more productively negotiating a monetary cap on the amount of the indemnity.

Fortunately, when the session resumed, we did manage to work out a deal, and Charlie stayed pretty quiet.

Several months later, the vice president of Charlie's company sent my boss a letter of commendation about my negotiating skill, and privately called to offer me Charlie's job.

When you stay grounded in the moment, open, and conscious of your boundaries, displaying empathy and compassion for your negotiation partner, anger will not be able to uproot you or the negotiations.

CHAPTER 24

Be Patient

In negotiations, responding to anger—or any strong emotion—with patience can often lead to a successful resolution.

This is one of the lessons of the multiparty negotiations that culminated in the signing of the Northern Ireland Peace Accord, known as the Belfast Peace Agreement, in 1998. These negotiations were led by George J. Mitchell, the U.S. senator who served as the independent chairman of the process. His job was to manage ten political parties, two governments, decades of hostility and mistrust between Catholics and Protestants—and between Unionists and Nationalists—and the constant threat of terrorist sabotage. Senator Mitchell had his hands full.

Even before the talks got started, the two main Unionist parties criticized the unelected chairman for having been foisted upon the group by the Irish and British governments. On the first day, one of the Unionist leaders repeated "no, no, no" the moment that Mitchell took his seat; soon afterward, both leaders led their members out.

The senator stayed calm, however, gave his opening statement, and pledged to work fairly and impartially for peace and political stability in Northern Ireland.

Next he announced the principles of democracy and non-violence that came to be known as the Mitchell Principles and proposed that each party affirm its commitment to them. All present did so.

Mitchell then had to convince the two Unionist groups to come back to the table and accept the principles. If they refused, he told them they would be ineligible to participate. Here he was able to separate the issue (the U.S., British, and Irish governments ostensibly colluding against the Unionist groups) from the person leading the process (who the Unionists saw as a puppet of that supposed alliance). Mitchell didn't take their rebuff personally. He realized that his best course of action was not in what he said—"I will be fair and impartial"—but in what he did.

After some patient and protracted persuasion from Mitchell, the Unionists did return to negotiations and accept the principles. However, they continued to reject Mitchell as the leader of the process, refusing to acknowledge his authority or call him Mr. Chairman. Mitchell ignored this. In doing so, he not only stayed grounded and in the moment, but he also managed to keep his ego from getting intertwined with his goals.

The personal rebuff was not a rejection of his position; conversely, when the Unionists rejected his position, he didn't let it bruise his ego.

Over time, as Mitchell moved the issues forward with respect and understanding, they came to call him Senator, then Mr. Chairman, and finally, after seeing what Mitchell was made of, George.

Violence ended up temporarily derailing the process many times over the three-year negotiation. Nevertheless, all the parties remained committed to the principle of resolving their issues in a nonviolent manner.

By setting up the Mitchell principles as ground rules at the beginning of the negotiations, the senator was able to minimize the effect of terrorism that had become a way of life in Ireland. When a bomb exploded and the IRA claimed credit, the Sinn Fenn was expelled from the talks and not permitted to re-enter until they arranged for a continuous cease-fire by the IRA over a period of months.

Mitchell had learned the need for patience and tenacity years earlier, in an intense senate race in Maine. He was also able to analyze the situation calmly, see the broader perspective, and genuinely listen to all parties with compassion. The result was a transformative negotiation, a signed agreement, and lasting success.

CHAPTER 25

Influence by Educating

When I first went to work for Sun Microsystems in the late 1980s, we had a written policy prohibiting discrimination on the basis of sexual orientation. Although the fight to add sexual orientation to the written anti-discrimination policy had lasted several years, I was pleased to see that Sun had come out at the forefront on this issue. Many Silicon Valley companies still had not seen fit to protect their gay and lesbian employees against unequal treatment.

Nevertheless, Sun's health plan did discriminate by offering comprehensive benefits to its married heterosexual employees but not to gay, lesbian, and non-married heterosexual couples. I joined a small group of employees that had been negotiating for inclusion of domestic partner benefits in the health plan. Collectively, we devised a negotiation strategy that centered on education. The Buddha taught us that ignorance and fear are forms of aversion, and aversion causes suffering. Knowledge can dispel ignorance and fear, and thus contribute to achieving positive outcomes in transformative negotiations.

We recognized from the outset that the hardest part of the battle would be to win over hearts and minds, and to change people's ideas about homosexuality. All of Sun's top executives were men. Some were unaware of the prevalence of homosexuality; some were afraid of it; a few were downright homophobic. Several had big misconceptions about gay men in particular.

Our challenge was to educate the members of the executive committee—the body that voted on changes to the health plan—one person at a time.

The committee had two main reasons for not extending health benefits beyond married heterosexuals. The first was that covering AIDS-related illness would be prohibitively expensive. This was a red herring based on stereotypes. Gay men weren't the only people who got infected with HIV.

We gathered statistics and presented a position paper to the committee, showing that costs would be minimal, since coverage would not apply to pre-existing conditions. We pointed out that maternity leave and the expense of childbirth, covered for every female employee or spouse of a male employee, was just as costly as covering the smaller universe of HIV-positive employees.

The second reason for not extending benefits was that Sun's right-leaning investors, suppliers, shareholders, and employees would object to the company opening the door to its gay and lesbian employees in this manner. *So what?* we countered. Since when is doing the right thing contingent on keeping a small splinter group of extremists happy? Would we deny other minority groups equal rights if racists or sexists were unhappy?

Besides, Sun already had a policy not to discriminate. Now it was simply a matter of synchronizing the words on paper with the company's deeds.

We provided the committee with a list of other Bay-area companies that had already extended these benefits to gay and lesbian couples.

But by far the most effective way we educated the executive committee was through a letter from a high-level engineer who was gay and HIV-positive (I'll call him Nathan). He wrote passionately about his contributions to the company over the years and his feelings of frustration at not being treated fairly. And he stressed that he could not afford to wait two more years—the time it had taken to get Sun's general discrimination policy revised. The executives all knew this man, his abilities as an engineer, and his value to the company. After we had educated them about the issue in general, Nathan humanized it for them.

As a result, we were able to move the debate away from subjective ideas about individual morality, and focus Sun's leadership on what was good for the company—in this case, higher employee productivity through valuing and protecting everyone's health. Education also served to reframe the issue.

Soon thereafter, the executive board voted to offer domestic partner benefits to all couples, as part of a major HMO overhaul. Employees now could choose how to allocate and spend their insurance dollars. In this way Sun quietly validated the anti-discrimination policy and earned the gratitude and respect of its gay and lesbian employees.

CHAPTER 26

Persevere

Veteran authors recount horror stories of trying to publish a book. It has always been rather tough. Robert Pirsig sent the manuscript of his first book, *Zen and the Art of Motorcycle Maintenance*, to 107 publishers before he got an offer of publication. The 1974 title went on to become one of the best-selling volumes in history.

There will come a time in many negotiations when you'll want to call it quits. It's simply not going well, or you feel that you've given up too much, or the people involved have become angry and defensive. Maybe you're just plain tired, or it's taking too long and seemingly not worth the effort anymore.

My advice is to stick with it, until and unless it's clear that no acceptable deal is possible. As Vince Bugliosi says, "Winning is often simply getting up from the ground one more time than your opponent."[33] So do just that: Keep getting up from the ground until there is nothing worth getting up for. (Then get up and leave.)

Resilience and tenacity pay off.

Perseverance pays off. It can overcome a mountain of rejections. It can often outmaneuver financial or political advantage, or even superior leverage.

Senator Mitchell displayed this kind of perseverance in negotiating for the Belfast accord. No matter what setbacks arose during the three-year negotiation period—personal insults, walkouts, bombs going off—he adhered to his principles and kept the negotiations moving forward.

The Tewa Tribe exemplified perseverance in its six-decade negotiations with the U.S. government to regain their title to the sacred Blue Lake watershed. They stayed aware of changes in authority; built trusting relationships with key partners; used leverage wherever they could find it; and, through it all, never wavered from their goal.

Here's another example, from former Secretary of State Condoleezza Rice's memoir *No Higher Honor*. In the summer of 2005, the U.S. government was negotiating a framework agreement to end the nuclear trade moratorium with India. The United States wanted to assist India with its civil nuclear program in exchange for access to Indian technology and know-how. The potential framework had many critics, both inside and outside the two governments.

After months of groundwork, the parties began negotiating face-to-face in Washington. Then Rice's counterpart, the Indian foreign minister, told her that he could not get his prime minister to agree to the deal.

Rice had believed that the foreign minister had the authority to speak for his government, but apparently he didn't; moreover, the pressure back in India was decidedly against a deal with the United States.

Refusing to let the deal fail, she asked the foreign minister to set up a meeting for her with the prime minister. He said "no." She did not accept this answer. She continued to press the foreign minister for the meeting. After several attempts, he relented and was able to arrange it.

At this meeting, Rice urged Prime Minister Singh to think about the momentous opportunity to put Indian-U.S. relations on a fundamentally new footing. He pushed back, but finally agreed to instruct his key people to attempt to negotiate a deal one final time.

It took three more years—and several brushes with failure—but the framework agreement was ultimately ratified by both governments and the international nuclear community, thus making way for a final cooperative agreement to be negotiated.

As Calvin Coolidge, our thirtieth president, once said, "Nothing in the world can take the place of [p]ersistence. Talent will not; nothing is more common than unsuccessful [people] with talent. Genius will not; unrewarded genius is almost a proverb. Education will not; the world is full of educated derelicts. Persistence and determination alone are omnipotent. The slogan 'Press On' has solved and always will solve the problems of the human race."

CHAPTER 27

Leave the Past Behind

Why is it so hard to achieve peace between Israel and Palestine?

The groups have spent thousands of years fighting wars, burning temples, building walls, and persecuting peoples. Leaders have come and gone; negotiations have started and stopped, concluded and been reversed. Promises have been made and broken.

You could argue that everything is wrong in the current negotiations: a failure to listen, emotionally charged speech, unrealistic expectations, divergent communications styles, cultural disparities, and a lack of trust. There is a feeling (on both sides) that the parties have never had equal bargaining power in the negotiations. And there is a deep well of negative emotions on each side.

In his seminal book *From Beirut to Jerusalem,* published in 1989, Thomas Friedman says that one key reason there has not been peace between Israelis and Palestinians is that both parties are locked into the past, validating their positions based on ancient evidence. Friedman argues that when parties are focused on *rights* they have derived from ancestral or historical grants, those rights become immutable, the issues non-negotiable, and the parties immovable.

In contrast, when parties focus on their *interests*, which are derived from present needs and limitations, those interests invite dialogue and compromise. This present-moment focus is the foundation of mindfulness practice and allows you to see what's in front of you, not what's behind you or on the horizon.

The past is a burdensome frame that rarely moves negotiation forward. It takes a focus on the present to do that. And it's only when negotiators are able to shift attention to the here and now that significant progress can be made.

The historic peace treaty signed in 1979 between Israel and Egypt culminated with Israeli Prime Minister Menachem Begin and Egyptian President Anwar Sadat shaking hands on television. The accord was possible because each leader let go of past positions and focused instead on present-moment interests. By detaching Egypt's ancient rights from its present interests, Sadat created space for the Israelis to make decisions based on their interests, instead of on making peace with Egypt. Sadat was open; he let go of his old mind-set and was no longer ruled by the past. By changing his way of thinking about Israel, he was able to stimulate progress in the negotiations.

Begin also shed his traditional way of thinking to accept the land-for-peace blueprint as a means of resolving the Israeli-Arab conflict. At Camp David, in exchange for peace with Egypt, Begin legitimized the Palestinian people and affirmed their right to set up a transitional self-government in the West Bank and Gaza Strip, after which final status on these territories would be negotiated. In the process, he was transformed from a bellicose zealot into a Nobel Laureate statesman.

Sadat gave Israel psychological space by recognizing its statehood. Israelis, Thomas Freidman argues, need to do the same for the Palestinians. This will create the opportunity for Palestinians to stop focusing on their rights and to start making decisions based on their interests.

Twenty years later, the Oslo plan and Wye River accords brought the two parties one step closer to settling their disputes. In his book *The Process: 1,100 Days That Changed the Middle East,* Uri Savir, chief negotiator for Israel, describes how difficult it was to sit down with his counterpart, Ahmed Qurei (Abu Ala), the chief Palestinian negotiator. The two tough-minded men initially disagreed on everything; but eventually, as trust developed over the three-year negotiation, they became friends.

In the process, supported by the bold actions of three leaders—Yitzhak Rabin, Shimon Peres, and Yasser Arafat—the negotiators were able to address the present-day needs of their peoples, even while they remained suspicious of each other's motives. As Savir describes:

> The process, in fact, created a basic *interdependence* on the ground that made it impossible for either side to ignore or dismiss the other side without suffering consequences. A quasi-independent Palestinian government was responsible for its people, for the first time in their history, yet it depended upon Israel for their well-being. An Israel that had relinquished its full control over the Palestinians was dependent upon their cooperation to maintain one of its key interests: security. The economic prosperity of both sides also depended on peace.[34] (emphasis mine)

155

Savir offers an invaluable lesson about the interdependence of all things. The Palestinians and Israelis are one people in a shared territory, dependent on each other for survival. Once both parties can adhere to this core principle, and agree to abide by it, negotiations can proceed. This is a key component of transformative negotiations.

Try This:

Think of a difficult negotiation and identify your negotiating partner's past behaviors (or harms) that may have been an obstacle to present-moment focus. Write them down.

Now, practice cultivating compassion for the person you believe has harmed you by trying to understand the root of the person's suffering that may have caused the behavior. Is there any place where you might also have been to blame?

Next, separate the acts from the person and practice forgiving that person (in contrast to the person's behavior/actions), and letting go of the harm or past behavior. This can be done with breathing meditation and repeating the phrase "I forgive you for . . ."

What else would it take for you to be able move any future negotiations away from the past and into the present?

You can also try this when seeking forgiveness for harm that you may have caused to others.

The relationship between the United States and Iran is a prime example of the past blocking positive negotiations on present-day issues. As Ambassador John Limbert notes in his *Special Report 199*, "The American side is no more likely to overlook the wounds of the 1979-81 hostage crisis than is the Iranian side likely to put aside the memories of the 1953 CIA-sponsored coup against the Mossadegh regime."[35] These harms are real, but at the same time holding on to them prevents negotiators from focusing on creating agreements in the present.

The *Special Report* offers fifteen points for negotiating with the Iranian government that closely parallel many of the elements I've focused on in this book—including being prepared, building relationships, and knowing both your own and the other party's goals and real interests. Limbert concludes that an American negotiator must remain patient and focused not on past grievances, but on present interests.

CHAPTER 28

Embrace the Present; Move into the Future

A negotiator can see the universe in one of two ways: as many separate, distinct parts randomly thrown together, or as one unified whole.

The separation approach leads to trying to gain or retain control in negotiations. The unified approach recognizes that every action has a universal dimension.

When we negotiate using this unified approach, we abandon our egos but not our goals. The negotiation conducts itself, and we see the individual actors as vehicles through which energy flows.

I've experienced this firsthand. When a negotiation is going well, it's happening on its own.

In contrast, when a negotiation is blocked, I'm very aware of my self in the equation. Sometimes I lose my connection with universal energy and have to deliberately reestablish it.

Some people do this through meditation, or deep mindful breathing, or time alone, often in nature. I do it by practicing what is called *qigong,* an internal martial art that consists of slow movements to activate *qi* (life force) in the body. Pulling *qi* from the earth and the heavens, and mingling it with my *qi,* I feel the energy in my own microcosmic universe fed by the energies around me. Connection on this level supports my intuition. I can sense the world moving through me. I can also sense when things are out of balance.

When you negotiate in an interdependent way, as part of the universe, you are open and vulnerable. You naturally practice humility, act beyond narrow self-interest, and strive for commonality. As the Dalai Lama puts it, "This self-other overlap is considered to be the basic, undifferentiated core of all these beneficial effects, as it is difficult to be biased, prejudiced violent, etc. if you see the other as being the same person as you are—in a partial, psychological way at least."[36]

This unified approach to negotiation reminds us that we can't separate from each other. It also reminds us that we can't separate today's actions from our future. Some people call this *consequences* or *outcomes*; others refer to it as *karma.* Goldstein brings them both together when he points out that karma is the understanding that as human beings, we can only truly claim responsibility for our actions and their results. "When we integrate this realization into our lives, we pay more attention to our choices and actions, and to where they are leading."[37]

The way a negotiation is conducted is a fairly good predictor of the way the relationship will play out if both parties come to agreement. Certainly, energy of the negotiations, whether positive or negative, spills over into the subsequent relationship.

It's also true that the way your negotiation partner (or their organization) treats you today is likely to represent how they will treat you tomorrow or the next day. A strong foundation in the present helps create a positive future.

We must constantly be aware of the costs and consequences of our negotiating behavior. For example, if you try to extract more than your partner can live with, you might gain something in the short run, but cause resentment that lingers long after the deal is concluded. Sometimes, rather than lose goodwill, you might be wise to settle for a bit less, so that your negotiation partner feels reasonably satisfied.

When you negotiate with strength, leverage, humility, empathy, respect, and fairness, fully aware of the cause and effects of your actions, you increase the likelihood of achieving success—both in the current negotiation and in future ones.

If you try to deny someone else the satisfaction of a reasonable bargain, you are essentially stealing from them, the universe, and yourself. The candidate interviewing for a job who insists on an unrealistic salary; a person who uses unequal bargaining power to extract unnecessary concessions from a neighbor just because he or she can; the CEO who imposes an impossible delivery date—all of these negotiations will ultimately fail in the end, even if the deals are consummated. The employer who agrees to pay an exorbitant salary may mistrust the employee's loyalty. The neighbor who was backed into a corner may become an enemy instead of a friend. The vendor who agrees to the impossible delivery date will either miss it or become utterly exhausted while working to meet it.

All of these outcomes can be avoided by simply paying attention to the consequences of present actions.

When we ignore the rest of the universe and focus solely on our self-interest, we find ourselves caught in a web we didn't even realize had been woven. But when we negotiate with the entire cosmos sitting at the table, we can move toward agreement as smoothly and as speedily as possible.

CONCLUSION

Transformation

One year, for my birthday, I wanted to do something novel. So I crossed the Brooklyn Bridge on foot.

The bridge was conceived in the mid-1800s. It's a wonder of architectural and graphic design, with a web of thick steel cables and two Gothic towers. It took the designer and engineer, John Roebling, nearly thirty years to realize his dream of spanning the East River between New York and Brooklyn. The project didn't get started until 1867 when money was finally appropriated by the legislature and Roebling was named engineer. Nearly two years into the project, he crushed his leg between some dock pilings and a ferryboat. He died of tetanus three weeks later.

His son Washington took over the project, only to suffer nerve damage during an underwater accident that left him confined to a wheelchair. He sat in his Brooklyn Heights house and watched the construction through a telescope, sending his wife down with instructions and drawings to supervise the remainder of the job. Washington himself never set foot on the structure, which took shape only through the actions of other able-bodied people.

The bridge was opened in 1883, sixteen years after John Roebling first began designing the project and twenty-six years from the time that his first rudimentary drawings of towers holding cables took shape in the mid-1850s. The story of the Brooklyn Bridge is a prime lesson in perseverance.

I stepped onto the promenade, a path elevated slightly above the roadway. It was crowded with runners, camera-toting tourists, and New Yorkers on Rollerblades.

Close up, the bridge was awesome. Each steel cable was as thick as a human being. As I walked slowly across, I was mesmerized by a structure I had lived with for years, but had never bothered to get to know.

The most startling part of my odyssey was turning around to face an exquisite view of Manhattan at sunrise. In all my years on that congested island, it never dawned on me to look at my birthplace from this vantage point.

Seeing Manhattan as an island with many connections gave me something much greater than a simple change in optics, frame, or perspective. Suddenly, I had a fundamentally different orientation. The view transformed me.

More recently, I traveled to East Africa. I spent ten days in wildlife preserves, observing animals without bars between us, and walked across the Serengeti plains with spear-carrying Masai warriors as guides. In Tanzania, the horizon is so expansive you can't help but be stretched to meet it. And sleeping in a tent among the lions, wildebeest, and hyenas changes your point of reference in terms of personal safety.

The last part of our trip was a long drive to meet with a

tribe of nomadic people, the Hadza. Just finding their camp was difficult and dangerous. By the time we arrived, we were tired and broken open. Communicating with tribal members was challenging, as none of the Hadza spoke anything other than their traditional clicking language.

We joined the men as they hunted for honey. They called out to birds that lived in a certain species of tree. The birds called back, helping them locate the right trees. The honey was harvested from inside the bark and consumed immediately. With the women, we learned to dig for tubers, then cleaned and cooked them over a makeshift fire for a shared lunch. We watched how they made bows out of bushes, pounding the crooked branches into shape. We played a gambling game that involved throwing pieces of bark at the root of a tree; we bet pencils and T-shirts, and the Hadza bet untipped arrows.

This way of life was a study in present-moment living.

Living among the Hadza was a life-changing experience. These people had nothing but the clothes on their backs, but they were happy. And it felt good to know that a portion of the money we spent on that leg of the trip went to help the Hadza in a legal battle to retain their ancestral lands.

If you're not able to transform your thinking by leaving a room, crossing a bridge, or visiting a foreign land, try simply changing your routines or your internal frame of reference. Get used to expanding rather than contracting in the presence of anything new, unfamiliar, or unknown. This will also help you naturally expand rather than contract in negotiations.

The negotiating techniques we have explored together all have transformational aspects. They can change us, our negotiation partners, and the world in profound and positive ways. Every time you actively listen to your partner, or speak with clarity, or adopt a broad perspective, or set aside your ego, you are effecting change.

Remember the value of being authentic in negotiations. Know yourself, and work to know and understand your negotiation partner. This includes exploring not only what each of you needs from the negotiation, but why each of you is negotiating.

Each negotiation is an opportunity to be prepared, present, and assertive; to extend compassion, fairness, and kindness to others and to yourself; and, of course, to achieve your goals and satisfy your wants or needs, without sacrificing those of your negotiation partner.

Practice humility, patience, and perseverance. These are the most important tools of a transformative negotiator.

In this we way can transform the world, one negotiation at a time.

Notes

1. Robert Bolton, *People Skills: How to Assert Yourself, Listen to Others, and Resolve Conflicts* (New York: Simon and Schuster, 1979), 61.

2. Joseph Goldstein, *Mindfulness: A Practical Guide to Awakening* (Boulder: CO: Sounds True, 2013), 376.

3. Deborah Tannen, *That's Not What I Meant! How Conversational Style Makes or Breaks Relationships* (New York: Ballantine, 1986), 91.

4. Walter Isaacson, *Steve Jobs* (New York: Simon & Schuster, 2011), 434-35.

5. Jon M. Huntsman, *Winners Never Cheat: Everyday Values We Learned as Children (But May Have Forgotten)* (New Jersey: Pearson Prentice Hall, 2005), 117.

6. Matsumoto Michihiro, *The Unspoken Way* (New York: Kodansha, 1988), 43.

7. Robert M. March *The Japanese Negotiator: Subtlety and Strategy Beyond Western Logic* (New York: Kodansha, 1988), 78–79.

8. Louann Brizendine, *The Female Brain* (New York: Broadway Books, 2006).

9. Fiona Grieg, *A Fresh Look Through the Glass Ceiling*, Harvard Law School Negotiation newsletter, 2011.

10. Sheryl Sandberg, *Lean In: Women, Work, and the Will to Lead* (New York: Random House, 2013), 47.

11. Laura J. Kray, Jessica A. Kennedy, and Alex B. Van Zant, "Not Competent Enough to Know the Difference: Gender Stereotypes about Women's Ease of Being Misled Predict Negotiator Deception," *Organizational Behavior and Human Decision Processes* 2014, http://dx.doi.org/10.1016/j.obhdp.2014.06.002.

12. Condelezza Rice, "Transformational Diplomacy" (lecture, Georgetown School of Foreign Service, January 18, 2006), http://2001-2009.state.gov/secretary/rm/2006/59306.htm.

13. Dalai Lama, *The Art of Happiness in a Troubled World* (New York: Doubleday, 1998), 232.

14. Shawn Achor, *The Happiness Advantage: The Seven Principles of Positive Psychology That Fuel Success and Performance at Work* (New York: Crown Books, 2010), 46 (citing a study by S. Kopelman, A. S. Rosette, and L. Thompson, "The Three Faces of Eve: Strategic Displays of Positive, Negative, and Neutral Emotions in Negotiations," *Organizational Behavior and Human Decision Process* 99 [2006]: 81–101).

15. Pierre Salinger, *America Held Hostage: The Secret Negotiations* (New York: Doubleday & Co., 1981), 130.

16. Bryan Burrough and John Helyar, *Barbarians at the Gate: The Fall of RJR Nabisco* (New York: HarperCollins,1990), 331

17. Herb Cohen, *You Can Negotiate Anything* (New York: Bantam, 1982), 31.

18. Edward de Bono, *I Am Right—You Are Wrong* (New York: Viking, 1990), 291.

19. Dalai Lama, *The Art of Happiness*, 143.

20. Michihiro, *Unspoken Way*, 37

21. Ibid., 102–103.

22. Ibid., 51.

23. This story is discussed in Marvin Kalb and Bernard Kalb, *Kissinger* (Boston: Little, Brown & Company, 1974).

24. Ibid., 357.

25. Huntsman, *Winners Never Cheat*, 34.

26. Kalb and Kalb, *Kissinger*, 137.

27. Salinger, *America Held Hostage*, 130.

28. Fred Lager, *Ben & Jerry's: The Inside Scoop* (New York: Crown, 1994).

29. Lothar Katz, *Negotiating International Business: The Negotiator's Reference Guide to 50 Countries around the World* (Charleston, SC: BookSurge, 2006).

30. Steven M. R. Covey with Rebecca R. Merrill, *The Speed of Trust: The One Thing That Changes Everything* (New York: Free Press, 2006), 64.

31. Walter Isaacson, *Benjamin Franklin: An American Life* (New York: Simon & Schuster, 2003), 491.

32. Goldstein, *Mindfulness*, 361–62.

33. Vincent Bugliosi, *Outrage: The Five Reasons Why O.J. Simpson Got Away with Murder* (New York: W.W. Norton & Co., 1996), 128.

34. Uri Savir, *The Process: 1,100 Days That Changed the Middle East* (New York: Random House, 1998), 310.

35. John W. Limbert, *Negotiating with the Islamic Republic of Iran: Raising the Chances for Success—Fifteen Points to Remember.* Special Report 199 (Washington, DC: United States Institute of Peace, January 2008), 3.

36. Dalai Lama, *Art of Happiness*, 316.

37. Goldstein, *Mindfulness*, 351.

Bibliography and Suggested Reading

Achor, Shawn. *The Happiness Advantage: The Seven Principles of Positive Psychology That Fuel Success and Performance at Work.* New York: Crown Books, 2010.

Bolton, Robert. *People Skills.* New York: Simon & Schuster, 1979.

Brizendine, Louann. *The Female Brain.* New York: Broadway Books, 2006.

Buderi, Robert, and Gregory T. Huang. *Guanxi (The Art of Relationships): Microsoft, China, and Bill Gates's Plan to Win the Road Ahead.* New York: Simon & Schuster, 2006.

Bugliosi, Vincent. *Outrage: The Five Reasons Why O.J. Simpson Got Away with Murder.* New York: W.W. Norton & Co, 1996.

Burrough, Bryan, and John Helyar. *Barbarians at the Gate: The Fall of RJR Nabisco.* New York: HarperCollins, 1990.

Camp, James R. *Start with No... The Negotiating Tools That the Pros Don't Want You to Know.* (New York: Crown Business, 2002).

Cohen, Herb. *You Can Negotiate Anything.* New York: Bantam, 1982.

Covey, Steven M. R., with Rebecca R. Merrill. *The Speed of Trust: The One Thing That Changes Everything.* New York: Free Press, 2006.

Dalai Lama and Howard C. Cutler. *The Art of Happiness in a Troubled World.* New York: Doubleday, 2009.

de Bono, Edward. *I Am Right—You Are Wrong.* New York: Viking, 1990.

Faber, Adele, and Elaine Mazlish. *How To Talk So Kids Will Listen & Listen So Kids Will Talk.* New York: Avon, 1980.

Friedman, Thomas. *From Beirut to Jerusalem.* New York: Anchor Books/ Doubleday, 1989.

Gordon-McCutchan, R. C. *The Taos Indians and the Battle for Blue Lake.* Santa Fe: Red Crane Books, 1991.

Goldstein, Joseph. *Mindfulness: A Practical Guide to Awakening.* Boulder: Sounds True, 2013.

Grant, Adam. *Give and Take: Why Helping Others Drives our Success.* New York: Penguin, 2014

Hahn, Thich Nhat. *Old Path White Clouds: Walking in the Footsteps of the Buddha.* Berkeley: Parallax Press, 1991.

Howe, Neil, and William Strauss. *Generations: The History of America's Future, 1584 to 2069.*
New York: William Morrow & Co, 1991.

Huntsman, Jon M. *Winners Never Cheat: Everyday Values We Learned as Children (But May Have Forgotten).* New Jersey: Pearson Prentice Hall, 2005.

Isaacson, Walter. *Benjamin Franklin: An American Life.* New York: Simon & Schuster, 2003.

Kalb, Marvin, and Bernard Kalb. *Kissinger.* Boston: Little, Brown & Company, 1974.

Kissinger, Henry A. *Diplomacy.* New York: Simon & Schuster, 1994.

Lewis, Richard D. *When Cultures Collide: Leading Across Cultures.* 3rd ed. Boston: Nicholas Brealey Publishing, 2006.

Limbert, John W. *Negotiating with the Islamic Republic of Iran: Raising the Chances for Success—Fifteen Points to Remember.* Special Report 199. Washington, DC: United States Institute of Peace, January 2008.

March, Robert M. *The Japanese Negotiator: Subtlety and Strategy Beyond Western Logic.* New York: Kodansha, 1988.

Matsumoto, Michihiro. *The Unspoken Way.* New York: Kodansha, 1988.

Mitchell, George J. *Making Peace.* New York: Knopf, 1999.

Rice, Condelezza. *No Higher Honor: A Memoir of My Years in Washington.* New York: Crown, 2011.

Salinger, Pierre. *America Held Hostage.* New York: Doubleday & Co., 1981.

Savir, Uri. *The Process: 1,100 Days that Changed the Middle East.* New York: Random House, 1998.

Sinek, Simon. *Start with Why: How Great Leaders Inspire Everyone to Take Action.* New York: Penguin, 2009.

Tannen, Deborah. *That's Not What I Meant! How Conversational Style Makes or Breaks Relationships.* New York: Ballantine, 1986.

About the Author

Michèle Huff is an attorney who has negotiated on behalf of Fortune 500 companies, including Oracle Corporation, Sun Microsystems, and Canal+ and start-up companies, including Kalepa Networks and Cinnafilm. She has also negotiated on behalf of hundreds of individual clients and manages the Archer Law Group, a firm specializing in protecting and licensing creative properties.

Since 2008, she has been the University of New Mexico's lawyer for research, technology and intellectual property. She negotiates agreements with industry, academic institutions, and governmental agencies on a regular basis.

Michèle has taught intellectual property and licensing at the University of New Mexico's School of Law, and has led negotiation workshops for local community foundations, technology venture associations, and business incubators. In May, she co-presented a session on Transformative Negotiation at NBIA's 28th International Conference on Business Incubation in New Orleans. She was named one of Albuquerque Business First's 2014 Women of Influence.

Michèle's website is: www.michelehuff.com.

More Great Books from Unhooked Books

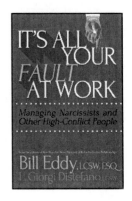

The Complicated Relationships Publisher

Available in paperback and in ebook (digital)
format from booksellers
everywhere

CPSIA information can be obtained at www.ICGtesting.com
Printed in the USA
LVOW10s0755161015

458520LV00001B/1/P